GW00471171

WAKE UP!

THIS IS IT!

THE GREAT APOCALYPSE!

THERE IS NOTHING HIDDEN THAT WILL NOT BE REVEALED!

EILEEN MCCOURT

Wake Up!

By Eileen McCourt

This book was first published in Great Britain in paperback during May 2023.

The moral right of Eileen McCourt is to be identified as the author of this work and has been asserted by her in accordance with the Copyright, Designs and Patents Act of 1988.

All rights are reserved and no part of this book may be produced or utilized in any format, or by any means, electronic or mechanical, including photocopying, recording or by any information storage or retrieval system, without prior permission in writing from the publishers - Coast & Country/Ads2life. ads2life@btinternet.com

All rights reserved.

ISBN: 979-8396141568

Copyright © May 2023 Eileen McCourt

CONTENTS

About the Author

Eileen McCourt is a retired school teacher of English and History with a Master's degree in History from University College Dublin.

She is also a Reiki Grand Master teacher and practitioner, having qualified in Ireland, England and Spain, and has introduced many of the newer modalities of Reiki healing energy into Ireland for the first time, from Spain and England. Eileen has qualified in England through the Lynda Bourne School of Enlightenment, and in Spain through the Spanish Federation of Reiki with Alessandra Rossin, Bienstar, Santa Eulalia, Ibiza.

Regular workshops and healing sessions are held in Elysium Wellness, Newry, County Down; New Moon Holistics N.I. Carrickfergus, County Antrim; Angel Times Limerick; Holistic Harmony Omagh, County Tyrone; Celtic School of Sound Healing, Swords, County Dublin; Kingdom Holistic Hub, Mill Road, Killorglin, County Kerry; Reiki Healing Bettystown, County Meath and Moonbeams, Carrigaline County Cork, where Eileen has been teaching the following to both practitioner and teacher levels:

- **Tibetan Usui Reiki levels 1, 2, 3 (Inner Master) 4 (teacher) and Grand Master**

- **Okuna Reiki (Atlantean and Lemurian)**

- **Karuna- Prakriti (Tibetan Usui and Hindu)**

- **Rahanni Celestial Healing**

- **Fire Spirit Reiki (Christ Consciousness and Holy Spirit)**

- Mother Mary Reiki

- Mary Magdalene Reiki

- Archangels Reiki

- Archangels Ascended Masters Reiki

- Reiki Seraphim

- Violet Flame Reiki

- Lemurian Crystal Reiki

- Golden Eagle Reiki (Native North American Indian)

- Golden Chalice Reiki

- Golden Rainbow Ray Reiki

- Goddesses of Light Reiki

- Unicorn Reiki

- Pegasus Reiki

- Elementals Reiki

- Dragon Reiki

- Dolphin Reiki

- Pyramid of Goddess Isis Reiki

- Kundalini Reiki

- Psychic Surgery

Details of all of these modalities can be found on Eileen's website, together with dates and venues of courses and workshops.

This is Eileen's 44*th* book.

Previous publications include:

- *'Living the Magic'*, **published** in December 2014

- *'This Great Awakening', September* 2015

- *'Spirit Calling! Are You Listening?', January* 2016

- *'Working With Spirit: A World of Healing'*, January 2016

- *'Life's But A Game! Go With The Flow!', March* 2016

- *'Rainbows, Angels and Unicorns!', April* 2016

- *'........And That's The Gospel Truth!', September* 2016

- *'The Almaculate Immaculate Deception! The Greatest Scam in History?',* September 2016

- *'Are Ye Not Gods?' The true inner meanings of Jesus' teachings and messages', March* 2017

- *'Jesus Lost and Found', July* 2017

- *'Behind Every Great Man........ Mary Magdalene Twin Flame of Jesus'*, July 2017

- *'Out of the Mind and into the Heart: Our Spiritual Journey with Mary Magdalene', August* 2017

- *'Divinely Designed: The Oneness of the Totality of ALL THAT IS'*, *January* 2018.   Also in **Audiobook**, May 2019

- *'Resurrection or Resuscitation? What really happened in That Tomb?'*, May 2018

- *'Music of the Spheres: Connecting to the Great Universal Consciousness and to ALL THAT IS through the music of Irish composer /pianist Pat McCourt'*, June 2018

- **'Chakras, Crystals, Colours and Drew the Dragon: A child's second Spiritual book'**, **July** 2018

- *'The Voice of a Master: It is Jesus Himself Who Speaks: Know Thyself'*, *December 2018*

- *'Kundalini', January 2019*

- *'Brave Little Star Child Comes To Earth'* - Audiobook- April 2019

- *'The Truth will set you free. - Christianity: Where did it all begin?'* May 2019

- *'Titus Flavius Josephus: Did Josephus write the gospels?'* June 2019

- *'Homo SPACIENS: We Are Not From Planet Earth! Our connection with UFOs, ETs and Ancient Civilisations'* August 2019

- *'Those Strange Looking Men In Their Flying Machines: Visitors From Beyond Time and Space? Or From Planet Earth? - ETs, UFOs and Who Knows What'* September 2019

- *'I Want to Break Free: Helping our Planet Earth ascend to a higher vibration of Love, Joy, Peace and Happiness for all. We can do it!'* November 2019

- *'The Universe is Mental! Understanding the 7 Spiritual Laws of the Universe, the Hermetic Principles that govern Creation'* January 2020

- *'To Be Or Not To Be.... The Man of Stratford who was never to be Shakespeare: Exposing the deception that was William Shakespeare' February* 2020

- *'If Not Shakespeare, Then Who? Unmasking the Real Bard of Avon! ' April* 2020

- *'What On Earth Is Happening? 2020: Year of Balance: Rise of the Divine Feminine' April* 2020

- *'Creating a New World! - Nature WILL be obeyed! - The greatest lesson never taught, but which we need to learn'* May 2020

- *'Humanity's Greatest Challenge? Breaking out of the vortex of ignorance and superstition' May* 2020

- *'Puppets on a String! But! The Strings have been broken! We are free!'* July 2020

- *'Out of the Darkness of Deception and Despair - into the Light of Truth',* February 2021

- *'Lighting the Way: A Little Magic Book of Spiritual Messages and Meanings', May* 2021

- *'Man in the Mirror: Reality or Illusion?'* July 2021

- *'Living Earth: Our Relationship with Mother Nature',* July 2021

- *'The Singing Soul', July* 2021

- *'Finding Sense in the Non-Sense: Seeing the greater picture',* September 2021

- *'Above Our Heads: Predators or Protectors? Extraterrestrials; - The best-kept secret now exposed?* - January 2022

- *'Changing your life - Living the Reiki Way - In Today's World! Just for Today...'* January 2022

- *'Dear God.......Where are you?......A Bewildered Soul Talks With God' -* February 2022

- *'You're just a number....and the Universe has it!'* May 2022

- *'Let Eriu Remember - Lessons and teachings embedded in myths and legends of our sacred sites'. -* November 2022

- *'Ancient Ancestors Calling! With words of wisdom and knowledge for today's world'.* - December 2022

and now this current book:

- *'Wake Up! This is it! The Great Apocalypse!'*

Podcasts for each of these 44 books can be viewed on Eileen's website and on her author page.

Eileen has also just recently re-published a series of 5 local history books under the title '***Finding Our Way Back***'. These were first published in the 1980s:

Book One: '***Strange Happenings'*** - a 1988 collection of local ghost stories and local cures and charms, collected by the students of Saint Patrick's College Armagh.

Book Two: '***Tell Me More, Grandad!'*** - a collection of school day memories collected from grandparents and great-grandparents in 1990.

Book Three: '***Gather In, Gather In',*** - a collection of children's games and rhymes, 1942-1943, by the late Mr. Paddy Hamill, collected from the pupils in Lislea No 2 Primary School 1939 to 1947 when Mr. Hamill was Principal.

Book Four: '***A Peep Into The Past: Armagh in Great-Granny's day'*** - Earlier maps of Armagh, explaining how Armagh got its street names, together with photographs of streets and shop-fronts in the early 20th century. Also included is information on schools and education in Armagh in the 19th Century; newspaper articles of interest from 1848; traders in Armagh in 1863 and markets and fairs in Armagh, - of which there were many!

Book Five: ***''The Poor Law And The Workhouse In Armagh 1838-1948'*** - prepared when Eileen was on secondment in the Public Record Office of Northern Ireland, 1980-1981, under the scholarship scheme provided for teachers by the Department of Education. The resulting publication was used in local schools for coursework for examination purposes. Primary sources include the Armagh workhouse registers and minute books, which are all held in the Northern Ireland Public Record Office in Belfast; government commissions and reports; annual reports of the Poor Law Commission for Ireland 1847-1921, and photographs of the inside and outside of Armagh workhouse, now part of Tower Hill Hospital, taken in 1989 by the late Mary Donnelly (nee Finn), Saint Patrick's College, Armagh.

The recent series of FB weekly videos, *'Our Great Awakening'*, together with the previous series *'The Nature of........'* with Eileen and Declan Quigley, Shamanic practitioner and teacher can also be viewed on Eileen's website and on YouTube, together with a series of healing meditations and Shamanic journeys.

Recent Full Moon Meditations with Declan Quigley, Jennifer Maddy and Brenda Murnaghan can be viewed on Eileen's YouTube channel, - access through website.

Eileen has also recorded 6 guided meditation CDs with her brother, composer/pianist Pat McCourt:

- *'Celestial Healing'*

- *'Celestial Presence'*

- *'Cleansing, energising and balancing the Chakras'*

- *'Ethereal Spirit' - Meditation on the 'I Am Presence'*

- *'Open the Door to Archangel Michael'*

- *'Healing with Archangel Raphael'*

Eileen's first DVD, *'Living the Magic'* features a live interview in which Eileen talks about matters Spiritual.

All publications are available from Amazon online and all publications and CDs are in Angel and Holistic centres around the country, as specified on website.

Please visit also the BLOG page on Eileen's website.

Website: www.celestialhealing8.co.uk

Author page: www.eileenmccourt.co.uk

YouTube channel:

https://www.youtube.com/channel/UChJPprUDnI9Eeu0IrRjGsqw

ACKNOWLEDGEMENTS

Book number *44!*

Thank you yet again to my publishers Dr. Steve Green and Don Hale OBE, for all their work and support, and without whom none of these books would ever actually materialise!

And of course, not forgetting all of you who are buying my books and CDs wherever in the world you are, and all who have taken the time to give me feed-back, and to write reviews for me, both in my books and on Amazon. You are greatly appreciated!

Thank you to all who attend my courses, workshops and meditation sessions, sharing your amazing energies, taking us on such wonderful journeys and through such amazing experiences! We are all so blessed!

And thank you to all of you who have been following me on Facebook. I sincerely hope the posts are bringing some comfort and help to you in these present rapidly changing times when so many people are paralysed with fear, anxiety and uncertainty.

But all is well! All is as it should be! The Earth and all in her and on her are moving into a higher energy vibration level - all are ascending!

And as always, I give thanks for all the great blessings that are constantly being sent our way in this wonderful, loving, abundant universe.

Namaste!

3rd May 2023

Foreword

This book has not been written to bring doom and gloom, despair, depression or negativity of any kind. Far from it! Rather, it has been written to try and get people to WAKE UP! To become aware of what is going on right now in every aspect of our lives!

Yes, there is and has been, for the last number of years, a massive AWAKENING process going on right throughout humanity. An AWAKENING both to the true nature of each and every one of us, to who and what we truly are, and an AWAKENING to what is going on all around us in this world.

But there is yet a large percentage of people who are still asleep - in a coma even! And a self-induced coma at that! - The proverbial ostrich act! Escapism! Denial!

Escapism from what? In denial about what?

In denial about this decimated, divided and alienated world in which we now find ourselves. In the mistaken belief that if we do not see or hear or know about something, then it is not happening, and so we do not have to deal with it. Or if we do know and still ignore it, somehow it will all go away.

Or blind obedience! Blind obedience being simply avoiding having to think for oneself! And blind obedience is no excuse for not knowing the truth! It was Oscar Wilde who wrote, in 1891, *'Disobedience, in the eyes of any one who has read history, is man's original virtue.'*

And as Mark Twain wrote:

'Whenever you find yourself on the side of the majority, it is time to reform (or pause and reflect).'

We each have a responsibility to search for and find the truth! Ignorance is never an excuse! And despite what many say, ignorance is NOT bliss! Nor can it ever be! But in most cases, unfortunately, people still choose to follow the road of blissful ignorance rather than deal with the inconvenience and difficulty of considering and incorporating new information into their thought process. - Falling victim to the propaganda, the conformed thoughts and dictates of society and those around them! - An easy option indeed! But **never** a good idea!

As Leo Tolstoy wrote:

'Wrong does not cease to be wrong because the majority share in it.'

Each and every one of us needs to keep our mind open and remain objective with everything in our life, and to never allow our emotions or personal bias to dictate our conclusions, thoughts or actions.

Each and every one of us needs to free our logical, rational mind from the chains that can limit our growth and our ability to see the bigger picture. It is our intuitive mind we need to use! As Albert Einstein wrote:

'The intuitive mind is a sacred gift and the rational mind is a faithful servant. We have created a society that honours the servant and has forgotten the gift.'

We have been conditioned and programmed through our antiquated, dogmatic and manipulating education systems to reject new ideas that in any way challenge the long-established tightly controlled narrative of the status-quo. And so we have a *'mental block'* when it comes to how we perceive reality and ourselves. For far too long now, we have based our understanding and perception of past and present events in our world on the word of a small group of elite so-called *'experts',* without questioning them or seeking any alternative theories or possibilities. And the result? The result is that we are now finding out that we have been lied to on a massive scale! And there is still a vast amount of evidence which, if brought into the light of day, would seriously challenge everything we have ever been taught! Hidden evidence, - deliberately hidden and concealed from us! In case we get to know too much! We have allowed ourselves to become the *'sheeples'* - the derogatory, dehumanising and degrading term used by the Elite ruling class when referring to us! Lambs to the slaughter! - That's what we are!

Sigmund Freud wrote:

'Most people do not really want freedom, because freedom involves responsibility, and most people are frightened of responsibility.'

But! *'There is nothing hidden that will not be revealed.'* These are the words echoed throughout most of the ancient texts and writings, and also in Mark 4:22, Luke 8:17 and Matthew 10:26.

And the truth is, - we are now living in these days of the Great Apocalypse!

And the true meaning of Apocalypse? It is NOT what we have been led to believe it to be! It is not the end of time, with destruction and devastation on a massive scale, where we are all hurtled into total oblivion!

Apocalypse simply means **Great Revelations.**

And these current great revelations are so far-reaching, so all-encompassing, so all- revealing, that they must surely be a WAKE-UP call for us all!

A WAKE-UP call to what exactly? -

A WAKE-UP call to make us think!

A WAKE-UP call to the fact that we have been lied to, we have been deceived, we have been manipulated, we have been exploited, we have been used, we have been taken for fools, we have been hood-winked, we have been moved about as pawns in other people's chess games.

And it is not because we are stupid! And why do I say this?

Well, look at it like this! The salesman comes to your door, trying to sell you something you neither like, need nor want. But guess what? You end up buying it! And when he goes away with your money, you ask yourself, *'How did that happen? What did I just do? Am I stupid or what?'*

No, you are NOT stupid. Rather, that salesman is just so skilled and expert at his job, - the job of selling stuff. After all, he has been taught and trained to do just this! He could sell ice to an Eskimo! And he knows exactly what words to use, what buttons of yours to press, - all to make you feel that you really want and need whatever it is he is trying to sell! He knows how to manipulate language as a mechanism of control! Control over you! To get you to buy!

And you take it all in! You fall for it again and again! Simply because your mind does not work like his!

And all these great revelations that are coming now in what is a tsunami, - they are all revealing that we have been constantly lied to and the truths have been hidden from us, - all as part of the hidden agenda of those who wish to control and exploit us for their own mercenary ends, and not for our welfare. Those in whom we placed our trust, believing they were working on our behalf, looking after us, looking out for us, helping us. Unfortunately, and as these revelations reveal, the only ones they are looking out for are themselves! And it is all now being projected onto a massive world screen! A painful lesson indeed for us to learn!

We need to just face it! - Each and every government is a corporation, a money-making institution, whose main aim is self-preservation. That's why presidents are not elected, as we are led to believe, but instead SELECTED! And they are selected because they will keep the system going, - the system that keeps the mass of people working day and night to sustain and maintain the Elite minority of millionaires and billionaires in their lavish lifestyles! Most people kept in their lowest state of energy to maintain the status quo here on Planet Earth!

There are none so blind as those who will not see. And equally, none so blind as those who see only what they want to see. Leonardo da Vinci wrote:

'There are three classes of people: Those who see, those who see when they are shown and those who do not see.'

Truth only comes to each one of us according to the extent of our openness and our readiness to open our eyes and face the truth.

And the good news in all of this? The good news is that once we know what has been going on, once we see the truth, once we see what has been hidden, and once we take our heads out of the sand, - then this whole masquerade, this whole farce, this whole gross deception, can come to an end. As the saying goes, - *'Give a man enough rope and he will hang himself!'* And it's true!

To quote Abraham Lincoln:

'You can fool some of the people all of the time, and all of the people some of the time, but you can not fool all of the people all of the time.'

In several of my previous books, I revealed many of the falsifications, lies and gross deceptions that permeate our lives and that are so relevant to us now. -

- **'Puppets On A String!'**

- **'Out of the Darkness of Deception and Despair, into the Light of Truth'**

- **'The Truth Will Set You Free: Christianity, - Where did it all begin?'**

- **'.....And That's the Gospel Truth'**

- **'The Almost Immaculate Deception'**

- **'Man in the Mirror'**

So there is no need to repeat those here. We are all swimming and floundering around in an ocean of falsifications, lies and gross deceptions.

But it is not for me, nor for anyone else, to tell you what you should or should not believe. Only you, and you alone, can decide that for yourself. To quote Socrates: *'I cannot teach anybody anything. I can only make them think.'*

And in this current book, **'WAKE UP!',** I cannot make you see the truth. I can present information to you, but how you receive it and react to it is always your own free choice. I can only hope to make you think! And when you start to think, then you begin to WAKE UP!

I do not claim to have all the answers. But that does not prevent me from asking the questions! Or from thinking! As Aristotle wrote:

'It is the mark of an educated mind to be able to entertain a thought without necessarily accepting it.'

And as Confucius wrote:

'The man who asks a question is a fool for a minute; the man who does not ask is a fool for life.'

The truth will come to each and every one of us when and as we are ready. Simply because every human being has a different level of consciousness, a different level of awareness. Which means simply that the ability to comprehend or understand complex or even straight-forward concepts and the bigger picture is different for each one of us. Becoming more consciously aware means that the individual has taken on the responsibility for himself to investigate and question everything we have been taught, everything we are being told, everything we read, - all in pursuit of finding and unearthing the truth.

And as you take on the truth, then you experience a rise in consciousness, an increase in awareness. It is then that you become AWAKENED! Happy days! As the Chinese philosopher Lao Tzu once said:

'The key to growth is the introduction of higher dimensions of consciousness into our awareness.'

We have each come into this third dimension dense energy-vibration level of Planet Earth in order to grow, - to grow through expanding our consciousness, through increasing our awareness. And we will never be able to do this as long as we continue to allow ourselves to be bound by the chains and fetters of false information, lies, gross distortions and manipulations. We need to WAKE UP! Because we need to understand that the future of us all as collective humanity is determined by the ability of each one of us to raise or expand our level of awareness or consciousness.

The satirist, Jonathan Swift wrote *'Gulliver's Travels',* a classic of English literature, as he himself claimed, *'to vex the world rather than divert it.'* Gulliver, the *'giant'* wakens up on a beach on which he has been shipwrecked, to find to his great alarm, that he cannot move. Gradually, he realises that while he has been asleep, an army of little *'Lilliputians'* has tied him down in a mass of silken threads.

A strong satirical message here with which increasing numbers of people can now resonate! While we have been asleep, others have been at work! And not for our good! Just like Gulliver, we have been tied in knots as we have been asleep! And now unable to move! Get the message?

And please note the *'silken threads'*. Not coarse, cutting ropes! But *'silken'* threads! Just like we are being given soft-spoken platitudes, euphemisms, appealing statements, - *'for your safety', 'for the good of the country', 'to keep us all safe'* etc. etc. etc.' All the softly-softly approach. And therein lies the cunning!

And you cannot say any longer that the truth has been kept from you! Here it is!

And yes! The truth is often painful! As Carl Jung wrote:

'There is no coming to consciousness without pain.'

And as Benjamin Franklin, one of the Founding Fathers of the United

States of America wrote:

'*We are all born ignorant, but one must work hard to remain stupid.*'

Certainly absolute ignorance and stupidity are endemic in our world!

Time to WAKE UP!

Chapter 1:

Man's natural essence

The greatest truth that has been hidden from us is the truth about our natural essence. The truth about our natural birth right!

We are essentially spiritual beings having a physical experience for the duration of this life-time. We are sparks of Divine Essence, Divine Energy, inherently embedded in the One Great Universal Energy, the One Great Universal Consciousness, the One Great Universal Awareness we call God, outside of which nothing and no person or any other form of life can possibly exist. We are all an inherent part of this One Universal God Energy, - a part of it and not apart from it. We are all in the Oneness, - there is no duality. God is not any sort of external figure. Nor does God belong to any religion, because God has nothing to do with religion.

God has got to do with Creating. That is what the God Energy does! It creates! That's it! And we, as humans, are God in physical manifestation, God as a physical creation. Each one of us is the God energy experiencing '*Itself*' *in* physical form. Each one of us is God, - and this is not some sort of spiritual arrogance, but merely an acceptance and an acknowledgement of our own natural essence. But no one of us is God in God's entirety. That's the essential difference! Rather, everything that has ever been, everything that is, and everything that ever will be, - all is combined in the One Great God Energy, - all of this is what constitutes the One Great God Energy. Together, we all make up God, together we all ARE God in God's entirety.

Just like when you think of the great ocean. If you dip your finger in the water and take out a single drop, that single drop on your finger has all the qualities of the entire ocean - the water element, the salty taste, - but that single little drop on your finger is not the ocean in the ocean's entirety.

Think too of the Cosmic hologram. When you cut any hologram up into tiny pieces, the entire hologram is still contained within each tiny piece! So each tiny piece is contained within the hologram and the entire hologram is contained within each tiny piece. The microcosm contained within the macrocosm and the macrocosm contained within the microcosm! And so it is for each one of us, - each one of us being a microcosm of the macrocosm, at the same time containing All That Is, and being contained within All That Is.

And All That Is, - that is energy. The One Great God Energy!

We are all energy. Everything is energy, vibrating on a particular energy vibration frequency, and the only difference between all the different forms of energy is the level of vibration frequency of each, - the rate or pace at which each different form is vibrating. That, and that only, is our means of identification when we pass back to Spirit at the end of this physical life-time.

Your soul is the over-all you. Everything you are, everything you ever have been and everything you ever will be. And in order to incarnate into this third-dimension energy physical world, we have had to dilute or step down some of our soul energy to enable us to take on physical mass or physical matter, - our physical bodies.

But we do not need to dilute ALL of our high energy, simply because first of all, our energy as beings of Light, is infinite, unending and eternal, and secondly, we do not need to drag along with us in this life-time all that we ever were before, - we need just enough to get us through this life-time. Our physical body is us in our diluted, stepped-down God Energy. The rest of our soul energy remains in the higher vibration levels, and this is what we call our Higher Self, - us in our undiluted, pure God Energy.

Our Higher Self, being each one of us in our undiluted God Energy, knows absolutely everything, - omniscient, omnipresent, omnipotent, omni-everything!

And we have access to our Higher Self at all times. So God is NOT any form of external figure. Rather God **IS** each one of us, and each one of us **IS** God in our Higher Self.

And when we pray, what exactly are we doing? We have been led to believe that when we pray we are praying to some external powerful figure who will grant some requests and withhold others, according to how hard and how often we pray! But such a figure just does not exist!

When we pray, we are connecting with our own Higher Self, and it is from here we get the guidance and the intuition we need.

Now I am not saying that we should not pray! Praying is positive and beneficial, because when we pray, we are usually praying for something good, so all that energy going out from us on a high frequency level, attracts the same energy back to us. And when we pray in large numbers, then that energy is magnified even more and comes back to us. That is the Great Universal Law! Irrefutable! Inviolate! Indisputable! Energy going out attracts the same back to us! What we give out, we get back! We reap what we sow! Or whatever other way you want to put it!

3

So continue to pray, by all means, but just be aware of what is actually happening when you pray! Be aware of the process that is taking place. The process of you connecting with your own Higher Self, your own pure undiluted God Essence, - your own natural essence!

And this has all been kept from us! We have been led to believe that we are all separate individuals, each of us following our own separate path, pursuing our own individual desires, without regard to anyone else. But we are NOT separate from everyone else! We are NOT separate from all other forms of life. We are NOT separate from Source, from ALL THAT IS. We are all in the collective 'WE'. We are all connected, there is no separateness. All of creation, in its entire totality, is connected. I am in you and you are in me. All the sky stuff, all the earth stuff, all forms of life, - all is one big living, pulsating, surging mass of energy. There is a certain degree of consciousness in everything, - in all that exists in the universe, in all that exists in the entire cosmos. And all consciousness communicates constantly and continuously on electro-magnetic frequencies, throughout all vibrational energy dimensions.

Our current belief that we are separate from all this universally combined energy, this belief which has been instilled into us, is a barrier to us seeing, accepting and therefore accessing the wholeness and entirety of existence. But all we are doing is disempowering ourselves, cutting ourselves off even further from the very Source that we need for our own existence.

And this individualistic, separateness thinking is what has led us to become the egotistical, greedy, competitive, capricious, envious creatures that we are, - harbouring negative, destructive thoughts of insecurity, suspicion, scarcity, envy, and the most negative of all, - fear!

We have been led to believe too that we are only this body. But we are NOT only this physical body! We are spiritual beings having a physical experience, and not physical beings having a spiritual experience.

And we have also been led to believe that God is a punishing figure, a deity on high, in male form, dictating our lives and meting out punishments to wayward, deviant, defiant humankind here on earth. And so we live in fear! A vast web of fear in which we all get caught up, entangled, strangled. Paralysed by fear! Because that is what fear does! It causes paralysis! It is fear that keeps us in bondage, suffocated by the dictates of those who arrogantly profess that their way is the only way.

And why have we never been taught the truth of our natural essence? Our natural God Essence! What we truly are!

Simply because this serves the interest of those who wish to control us! To control us, they need to disempower us! To make us feel inferior, insignificant, and to make us live in fear, - and so hand over our power to them! They will protect us! They will keep us safe! They will look out for us!

We have surrendered and given over our power! That ability and that right to think for ourselves!

Knowledge is power! And that is why knowledge of who and what we truly are has been kept from us! That is why we have been chained in the belief that we are only this physical body, and of course, sinners!

But Shakespeare's character Hamlet speaks of the beauty and capacity of man and his ability to transcend the limitations of the physical:

'What a piece of work is man! How noble in reason! How infinite in

faculty! In form and moving how express and admirable! In action how like an angel! In apprehension how like a god! The beauty of the world! The paragon of animals!'

And you have been led to believe you are only your body!

So, WAKE UP to who and what you truly are! - An infinite expression of consciousness, infinite awareness, infinite potentiality, pure God Essence! Cosmic travellers having an eternity of experiences throughout all time and space, and through all energy dimensions. Eternity is not something that begins with our physical death and goes on forever! THIS IS ETERNITY! THIS IS IT! This life-time is simply one of our endless walk-abouts, our endless journeys across time and space, all in pursuit of soul expansion.

And when you WAKE UP to who and what you truly are, then you can WAKE UP to what is happening in the world around you!

A decimated, divided and alienated world! But why?

Let us look!

Chapter 2:

A decimated, divided and alienated world

We have just seen how our natural essence is of the God Essence. And God is synonymous with Love. So we are Love.

War, violence, aggression, hate, envy, jealousy, - all of this is learned behaviour, foreign to our natural essence. Watch young children at play. They do not differentiate between skin colour, nationality, language or anything else. They all get on together and find ways to communicate despite language barriers. So all our aggression, prejudice, hatred and violence is something we learn as we grow older. Why?

On top of this, 99% of the world's people want peace, just to be allowed to live their lives in peace, happiness and joy, with good health, and to see their children and grandchildren grow up in a peaceful world.

Too much to ask? Too much to hope for? Too much to expect? - Why?

We all live in an abundant, self-replenishing Planet Earth, with plenty for everyone. Yet so many people are still living in poverty, hunger and destitution. And all this while many others live in luxury, with more money and wealth than they can ever spend. - Why?

Too much to ask, too much to hope for, too much to expect that everyone on this earth should have at least the basic necessities of life? - Why?

We are all One. All One within the One Great Universal Energy we call God. Each one of us is the Great Universal God Energy in physical manifestation, here on this earth plane for the sole purpose of soul expansion. And as we are all One, then everything is in each one of us, and each one of us is in everything. As we saw in the previous chapter, each one of us is a tiny microcosm of the macrocosm of entirety. Entirety being the cosmic hologram! And when you cut a hologram up into tiny separate pieces, each tiny piece still contains the entire hologram! So I am you and you are me!

So why then, if I am you and you are me, why are we all fighting against each other and killing each other? Why then is there so much racism, so much sexism, so many other negative 'isms' that are dividing us and keeping us apart? - Why?

Why is our world so decimated, so divided, so alienated? Why is peace constantly so elusive, when the vast majority of us want it? If our natural essence is Love, - and it is, - then why are so many people so full of hate, intolerance and prejudice? - Why?

So many questions! And the answers?

As we have already seen, racism is not natural. It is taught and learned. And the same with hatred and prejudice. Racism was simply an essential component of the process of colonialism down through history, and the acquiring of colonies for mercenary and imperial gain. In order to justify the land-grabbing colonial projects of earlier centuries, in the march of imperialism, it was necessary to create an ideology. To show that we, the Europeans, or the Americans, - or whoever, - have come to rescue the rest of the world from its depravity and backwardness. But in order to do that, it was necessary to demonstrate that the rest of the world was depraved and backward. And from this, arose the racism that is still so prevalent with us today. But we are all the one human family. We are all spiritual beings having a physical experience for the duration of this life-time. Each of us is an expression of infinite awareness, an infinite expression of consciousness, an unending stream of consciousness, having an eternity of experiences, and this life-time is only one of those experiences. We are all one and the same consciousness, just having different experiences within that one consciousness. I am not this body. I am not this black or white body. I am not a black or white person. Being black or white or whatever is just another experience, and this body is just the vehicle through which I can have that experience. I am eternal consciousness, infinite awareness, and I do not need to limit myself to this particular body, which is not the essence of me. Fighting and killing each other because of the colour of our skin is not natural. And yet we are doing it! - Why?

And when our natural essence is Love, when we live in a bountiful, self-replenishing Planet Earth, where there is plenty for everyone, and when 99% of the world's people just want to be left alone to get on with enjoying their lives in peace, then all this hatred, racism, violence, anger, war, etc., everything that is going on in our world right now, cannot be natural. And if it is not natural, then it must all be fabricated. Right? And if it is all fabricated, then there must be some person or persons doing the fabricating. Right again? - But why?

The answer to each one of these questions is the same! - Conditioning! Being made to believe that this is the way it is! This is how things are done! We are conditioned to focus our minds on poverty, want and suffering, so that is what we manifest. Our thoughts create our reality, and by focusing our attention on poverty and want, then that is what we are bringing into our lives.

I honestly believe that human nature is fundamentally and inherently loving and kind. Inherently good. And I honestly believe that in most cases, people will avoid conflict unless they are deliberately provoked or steered onto a violent path. War and violence is certainly indicative of an unevolved society, and as the natural path of our human evolutionary process is to a higher state of consciousness, then it appears to be obvious that something or someone is preventing our spiritual growth and our ascension to a higher state of being. This social conditioning where we are constantly in a state of war and conflict has been going on for so long now that we take it as normal. But the very opposite is the truth! We are deliberately being kept in a lower state of consciousness!

So the question is, who is fabricating all the war, violence and unrest in our world? If this is not the desire of 99% of us, then from where is it coming? Who wants to keep our world in war, violence and unrest? Who is pulling those strings? Who is controlling that agenda?

The answer? Obviously those who have a vested interest in maintaining war, violence and unrest! Those who have a vested interest in keeping us killing each other, keeping us in ill-health, keeping us in poverty, keeping us in fear. That small, tiny 1% of the world's population! So they, obviously, must be in control!

Why is there so much poverty, division, war and violence? They must be purposely created! There must be a reason for them! They must be being done on purpose! And they are!

But the question is by whom, and for what reason? Why are we being deliberately kept in a warring world, where poverty, violence and all that go along with these, are accepted as the norm, when they are not the norm, and when 99% of humanity do not want any of this?

War is everywhere! People against people, nation against nation, when we should all be together, all united against a common enemy. The common enemy, - those who lust for power and control, those who feed off the fear they instil into humanity. Just like in the movie *'Monsters Inc'*! The monsters are on a deliberate campaign to terrify the children. Why? Because the monsters need, as food for their survival, the negative dark energy that is emitted by the children as they experience extreme fear. A feast, life- sustenance, a life-source for the monsters!

Just as these escalating divisions between us, - these all lock us into the negative, low-energy vibrations that serve as energetic fodder for those who relish and thrive through constantly fuelling suffering, dis-ease, destruction and poverty. And as long as they can keep us trapped in this negative energy of fear, as long as they can keep us divided against ourselves instead of united, they can control, exploit and rule us! *DIVIDE AND CONQUER! DIVIDE AND RULE!* A strategy used right down through history! Deliberate provocation of division and conflict!

Everything is energy, everything is vibrating on a certain frequency, carrying a harmonious resonance, - high, positive bright energy, - or a disruptive resonance, - low, negative dark energy.

And there is a power game going on right now in front of our very eyes! A power struggle between the positive, high-energy forces of Love and the Light, and the lower, negative-energy forces of darkness. A battle of darkness and light! A battle for control of the soul of humanity. And those in power in our world are merely puppets, their strings being pulled by some form of control coming from another source. A source that remains covert, under the radar, secret, - as long as they have their cohorts, their minions, their fall-guys to work on the front line for them!

There are many who believe that we are moving from democracy into tyranny at an unprecedented rapid rate. They point to the unprecedented acceleration of totalitarian censorship, the unprecedented acceleration of mind control, the unprecedented acceleration of suppression of freedom and human rights, the unprecedented acceleration of violent suppression at peaceful demonstrations, the unprecedented acceleration of suppression of free thought and dialogue, the unprecedented acceleration of suppression of any sort of challenge to the dictates of those in power, those wielding the big stick of authority! The unprecedented acceleration of the watching all-seeing eye of Big Brother in every aspect of our lives! All of this has led us to where we now find ourselves, - this great divide between the people of our world, the extreme polarisation of perceptions, convictions, beliefs and ideologies. The extreme hatred and prejudice that is tearing us apart on every level! Extreme hatred and prejudice controlled, pushed and forced out to us constantly by mainstream media! Mainstream media which is nothing more than a propaganda machine for the Elite agenda! The Elite agenda to separate us and divide us, to tear families and friends apart, to force us into making life-altering choices, under threat of punishment and further alienation.

And unfortunately and sadly for humanity, many people are still totally unaware of it! Or even worse, denying it is happening! We are merely the pawns on the great world chessboard. Victims in the never-ending saga of abusive power, a system that keeps the working class working day and night to support the luxurious wealthy life-styles of those in power, - those who make the laws that sustain them in power, luxury and privilege. Those who make one set of rules and laws for us, to keep us in subordination, in servitude, in subjugation, and then another set of *'guidelines' for* themselves.

But the good news? The good news is that the more of us who WAKE UP, and realise what is going on, what games are being played out all around us, then those who are playing those games can no longer play them, - simply because they now know that we know! They know that all these revelations now continuing to pour out are exposing them! And that is taking the wind out of their sails! Their game is up!

Their game of keeping us a warring, divided world. A warring divided world simply to feed and sustain the big weapons and armaments industries who make their fortunes from promoting war and conflict - and then proceed to sell their weapons of mass destruction to both sides in the conflict. As the weapons industries in America did during World War Two, - selling at the same time to both the Allies and to the Nazis!

Their game of keeping us a world full of dis-ease, illness and sickness. A world full of ill-health simply to feed and sustain the big chemical and pharmaceutical companies who make their fortunes from promoting ill-health and sickness. Instead of targeting the problem at the source! - For example unclean water in so many parts of the world, unclean water that causes so many illnesses, - illnesses for which the pharmaceutical companies then offer pills, tablets and of course vaccinations!

These are 'The Military Industrial Complex' about which Truman, Eisenhower and Kennedy warned humanity!

So WAKE UP everyone! We are being ruled by those who do not wish to see a peaceful world or a healthy humanity!

WAKE UP!

Chapter 3:

Lies, lies and more lies

We have been lied to and deceived right down through history by our governments, by churches and religions, by big institutions, and by main-stream media.

Let us take history first.

It was Napoleon Bonaparte who said, '*What is history but a fable of agreed lies.*'

The French philosopher Voltaire wrote, '*History is a set of lies agreed upon.*'

And George Orwell, in his dystopian, or negative utopian novel, '*1984*' wrote: '*Who controls the past controls the future. Who controls the present controls the past.*'

Control of the past ensures control of the future, because the past can be treated essentially as a set of conditions, made to look like a set of conditions that are used to justify or encourage present or future aims or actions.

Orwell further wrote:

'*The further a society drifts from the truth, the more it will hate those who speak it.*'

And who writes the history books? The victors of course! The winners!

So history is full of bias, disinformation, lies, cover-ups and attempts to justify what has been done.

And the apparent principle is that it does not matter in the slightest whether what you are telling people is true or not! What matters is that you can convince them to BELIEVE it is true! It is their BELIEF that it is true that makes it true for them! Joseph Goebbels, Minister of Propaganda in Hitler's Third Reich, wrote:

'If you tell a lie big enough and keep repeating it, people will eventually come to believe it. The lie can be maintained only for such time as the State can shield the people from the political, economic and/or military consequences of the lie. It thus becomes vitally important for the State to use all of its powers to repress dissent, for the truth is the mortal enemy of the lie, and thus by extension, the truth is the greatest enemy of the State.'

Let me repeat that: *'The truth is the greatest enemy of the State.'*

And what more did Goebbels have to say?

'If you tell a lie big enough and keep repeating it, people will eventually come to believe it.'

And what massive lies have been told about both World Wars! About all wars indeed! - Vietnam, Korea, Afghanistan, Iraq, Ukraine! And of course the wars against the Native American and other indigenous peoples, and the conflicts in our own country here right down through history! It's always the same! Spin, spin and more spin, - to justify war and conflict, to *'dress up'* sinister actions. What is *'officially'* declared is never the truth!

And what person, what name in particular do we associate with both World Wars? Winston Churchill! The same Winston Churchill who has gone down in the history books as the *'saviour', the 'hero'* of Britain! One of the greatest ever!

The same Winston Churchill who declared:

'History will be kind to me, because I intend to write it!'

The same Winston Churchill who wrote:

'Man will occasionally stumble over the truth, but most of the time he will pick himself up and continue on.'

The very same Winston Churchill who said:

'You ask, what is our aim? I can answer in one word. It is victory, victory at all costs, victory in spite of all terror, victory, however long and hard the road may be; for without victory, there is no survival.'

Let me repeat: *'Victory at all costs'*.

And in his later book, *'The World Crisis', Churchill* wrote:

'The maneuver which brings an ally into the field is as serviceable as that which wins a great battle.'

And as David Sedgwick points out:

'This oft-quoted phrase draws attention to what could legitimately be termed our present culture of endemic dishonesty. We live at a time where deception may not only be tolerated, but providing it leads to the 'right' political outcomes ignored and tacitly encouraged. These first few decades of the twentieth century resounding to cries of 'fake news' may well become synonymous with an age of deceit, a lost weekend of

integrity and honour.' (David Sedgwick, *'The Fake News Factory'* page 18)

And what about Hitler? - The man we most associate with World War Two. What did he have to say?-

'Through clever and constant application of propaganda, people can be made to see paradise as hell and also the other way around, to consider the most wretched sort of life as paradise.' (*'Mein Kampf'* 1923)

And:

'How fortunate it is for governments that people do not think!'

And then of course we have, more recently, President Bill Clinton saying, when asked what was the most important consideration for any government? - *'It's the economy, stupid!'*

Yes, war is BIG, BIG, BIG business! And war and the economy are inextricably linked! It's all about money!

World War One! The *'War to end all wars'*! Yet within only 22 short years, the world was at war again! All part of government agenda! And why do I say, with such confidence and such certainty, that war is all part of government agenda? Well, straight from the horse's mouth! - President Franklin D. Roosevelt said:

'In politics, nothing happens by accident. If it happens, you can bet it was planned that way.'

Denis Healey, former British Labour Party Minister, who had previously served as the UK's Secretary of State for Defence, said:

*'World events do not occur by accident. They are made to happen,
whether it is to do with national issues or commerce; and most of them
are staged and managed by those who hold the purse strings.'*

And in the previous chapter, we saw how the one and only conclusion
one can come to about why wars come about, - despite the vast
majority of the world's people not wanting war, - is that war must be
deliberately being brought about. So we have just had confirmation that
it is! It's always part of the government agenda! Despite the lies they
continue to roll out and the vast war propaganda machine that tries to
tell us otherwise! The vast war propaganda machine that is rolled out to
manipulate people and make them think and do what the government
wants them to think and do. The vast war propaganda machine that is
used to sell war to young men, - depicting war as exciting, brave and
heroic! And of course, patriotic! The Motherland / Fatherland needs
you! What an honour to die for your country! This is the stuff of which
heroes are made! - Everything dressed up in euphemisms to make war
more attractive and appealing, and of course, justifiable! In World War
One, posters all encouraging young men to freely enlist, - all
propaganda promising them excitement, adventure, going to see the
world; the *'king's shilling'* that would keep the family going in coal and
food all winter; they would be *'home by Christmas'*; that grand new
uniform; all the lads in the street were enlisting, they were off to *'save
Europe';* they would return to a *'land fit for heroes'.*

And of course, when Belgium was invaded in 1914, - that was used too
as propaganda. *'Save poor Belgium!' 'A small country struggling to be
free!' 'Support the independence of small nations!' 'Do your duty!'*

Rich, and ironic, when we consider the vast sprawling British empire,
with colonies all over the world! And what about Ireland? Support the

independence of small nations? Another case of *'Do what I say and not as I do!'* See how the spin doctors can work it?

And the truth, what war really is, - killing fields, soldiers just fodder for cannon, - all kept from public consumption. The war poet Wilfred Owen in his most famous poem *'Dulce Et Decorum Est'* castigates the old saying about how brave and sweet it is to die for one's country, exposing it for what it truly is, - the *'old lie'*.

Owen's aim was to shock readers back home into the reality of the war, and having shocked them they would then no longer allow their young men to be sent out, not to honour and glory, but to the most horrific conditions and death imaginable.

And the truth more often than not does indeed shock!

Owen was the first to report the truth about World War One. The truth that was kept hidden from people back home. Simply because if that truth ever got out, no more men would join up. Letters from the soldiers to their folks back home were heavily censored, then reduced to merely a post-card-type, on which they simply ticked certain information, - for example: *'Everything good here'; 'Keeping well'; 'Be home soon'*, etc. etc. etc.

People back home led to believe that the war was going well. Going well, yes for the big military-industrial complex! Those who manufacture and sell weapons to keep their coffers over-flowing, - and selling weapons to both sides in the same conflict!

Government secret documents are kept secret for 30 years, and when that 30 years have expired, they can be kept for another 30 years. Then they must be disclosed, they must be fed into the public domain. Hence it is that we are now finding out a lot that we never knew before! And that what we were taught is not the truth! For example, how America came to enter World War One on the side of Britain.

We have always been taught about how the *'Lusitania',* a British passenger liner, en route from America to Liverpool, was sunk by a German u-boat torpedo, on May 7th 1915, off the Old Head of Kinsale, County Cork, Ireland, and how public outcry in America forced America into the war, as the *'Lusitania'* was carrying American passengers. A chance incident, a lucky chance incident for Britain, as it was vital that America enter the war on the side of the Allies? But as we are constantly being reminded, there is no such thing as chance or luck! Everything in politics has been planned! And everything that happens is inherent in the great Hermetic Principle of Cause and Effect!

The sinking of the *'Lusitania'* actually planned? The deaths of all those innocent people actually planned? A definite *'Yes'* to both questions. Fact! Sad but true!

And the truth? The *'Lusitania'* was, very suspiciously, travelling at a much slower speed than it should have been, in German U-boat-infested waters, where it should not have been, with no convoy as it should have had, it being a passenger liner. And what do we learn from the log book of the German submarine captain?

We learn that he fired only one torpedo. One torpedo was not enough to sink that ship. He left the scene and recorded that there was a second explosion, this one coming from within the *'Lusitania'* itself, next to the funnel. So what caused that second explosion? That was the explosion that sank that ship! But it was not caused by the torpedo from that German U-boat! Despite what we have always been told!

What does the Bill of Lading for the *'Lusitania'* tell us? It tells us that the *'Lusitania'* was carrying explosives, - 170 tons of rifle ammunition and 1,250 cases of artillery shells, as well as 50 barrels each of flammable aluminium and bronze powder. A supply of gun cotton! Guncotton, which is particularly lethal, as once salt water touches it, the whole thing explodes. And that is exactly what happened on the *'Lusitania'*. Carrying ammunition in war time made that ship a legal target for German U-boats. A sitting duck! A deliberate provocation! All planned!

And who planted that guncotton on board the *'Lusitania'*? Who was in charge of war operations? The very same Winston Churchill whom we have just considered. Winston Churchill! First Lord of the Admiralty! He who was absolutely determined to get America involved, as the Allies were fast running out of men. He who knew that American President Woodrow Wilson was reluctant to have America enter the war! This same Winston Churchill who, as we read earlier in this chapter, wanted *'victory at all costs',* and who stated, *'The maneuver which brings an ally into the field is as serviceable as that which wins a great battle.'*

Government documents now in the public domain clearly show that nothing was done to protect the *'Lusitania'* and its passengers. Earlier remarks made by Churchill implying that it would take a major disaster to get America into the war are very suspicious. The sinking of the *'Lusitania',* with many Americans on board, provided such a disaster.

So was the sinking of the *'Lusitania'* the result of deliberate action and planning on the part of Churchill? Or was it the result of deliberate inaction on the part of that same man? Deliberately taking no steps to secure the safe passage of the *'Lusitania'*? Churchill, the great warmonger! Churchill, the great war hero! Churchill, the saviour of Britain!

And what about Pearl Harbour, and the bombing by the Japanese of the entire American fleet, an action that once again brought America into a world war, this time into World War Two, again on the side of the Allies? How did the Japanese know that the American fleet would be berthed in that particular place at that particular time? Who leaked that information? Who set that up? Did Roosevelt attack Japan at Pearl Harbour? Was the attack on Pearl Harbour another example of myth masquerading as History?

And the Vietnam War? Another horrific scar on the face of humanity! A sustained and bloody battle to impose some decidedly Orwellian '*democracy*' on a sovereign state, - that '*raggedy-ass little country*' as President Lyndon Johnston called Vietnam.

The Gulf of Tonkin incident! August 1964. The incident that resulted in America's deep immersion into the Vietnam quagmire. US Navy Admiral George Stephen Morrison's allegation that he came under attack while patrolling Vietnam's Gulf of Tonkin. An allegation that was later proved untrue. An unprovoked attack on American ships by the Vietnamese, an '*attack*' that never actually took place! And the result? By early February 1965, the US, without a declaration of war and with no valid reason to wage one, - began indiscriminately bombing North Vietnam. By March of that same year, the infamous '*Rolling Thunder*' commenced. Over the course of the next three-and-a half years, millions of tons of bombs, missiles, rockets, incendiary devices and chemical warfare agents were indiscriminately dumped on the people of Vietnam in what can only be described as one of the worst crimes against humanity ever perpetrated on this planet.

In March of 1965, the first uniformed US soldier '*officially*' set foot on Vietnamese soil, although Special Forces units masquerading as '*advisers*' and '*trainers*' had been there for at least four years, and likely much longer. By April 1965, fully 25,000 uniformed American kids, most still teenagers barely out of high school, were slogging through the rice paddies of Vietnam. By the end of the year, US troop strength had surged to 200,000.

And the excuse given then? This was '*containing the spread of Communism*'! The most powerful country in the world engaged in war with one of the poorest? A war that dragged on for years after years? Now it is generally accepted that Vietnam was simply a testing ground for American weapons, in particular the lethal '*agent orange*'.

Let us move on now to the aftermath of World War Two. We have always been taught that the Nazi criminals were rounded up, tried and executed by a court in Nuremberg.

NOT TRUE! - More lies!

The Nazis were not defeated in World War Two, despite what the history books tell us! They simply re-located to America! They may have lost the fight, but they certainly won the peace! Many of the top brass Nazi officials were imported into America to work in the American space programme, and also into Russia. I have dealt with this specific, under-cover, secret '***Operation Paperclip***' in a previous book '***Those Strange Looking Men In Their Flying Machines: Visitors From Beyond Time And Space? Or From Planet Earth? - Ets, UFOs and Who Knows What.***' And also in the next chapter of this book.

War is always a means to an end! No war ever just happens! No country ever just '*drifts*' or '*slides*' into war! The early conflicts between the big empirical powers was all about snatching colonies to enhance their reputation, to increase their standing, power and influence in the world.

It had nothing to do with making life better for the conquered colonies, for bringing them *'civilisation'* or advancement of any kind, but everything to do with plundering and pillaging for supplies of raw materials, bringing those raw materials back to the *'Mother Country'*, producing material goods with them, and sending those same goods back to those colonies from which the raw materials had been extracted. So those colonies provided both a source of raw materials and a ready market for the finished goods. And that was the reason for all the big powers vying and competing with each other for colonies! The wealth that was to be had from the process! And wealth means power and prestige! - *'It's all about the economy, stupid!'*

The power in both world wars lay in the ability to develop war weapons on a mass scale, weapons that would kill and destroy the enemy. An enemy who was visible, and could be targeted. And now in this, the 21st century, we could be forgiven for having thought that those days were gone, gone for good. But no! - Reality check! Those days are still here, as seen in Afghanistan, Iraq, Syria, and now Ukraine. Weapons of mass destruction! - Weapons used to kill, kill, kill! Exterminate! Wipe off the face of the earth!

And not just that! This time we have the additional lethal weapon of FEAR!

Yes, it can be said, we are now in World War Three! But most people do not even know they are on a battlefield! A battlefield where the weapons are not only the conventional kind, where the enemy is seen or identifiable by a different colour of uniform or carrying a different banner! Oh no! The additional enemy in this World War Three is unseen, invisible! And it is not going for your body, but for your mind! This is psychological warfare, of the kind humanity has never known or experienced before.

Welcome to the 21st Century! Welcome to warfare in the 21st Century! Warfare which is mostly psychological and where the main weapon is fear!

Fear! That most negative energy! Paralysing! No missiles needed when you have the weapon of fear in your arsenal!

And Hermann Goering, the primary architect of the Nazi police state in Hitler's Third Reich! What was his reply when asked at his trial at Nuremberg how the German people came to accept everything?

'It was easy, it has nothing to do with Nazism, it has to do with human nature. You can do it in a Nazi, socialist, communist regime, in a monarchy and even in a democracy. The only thing that needs to be done to enslave people is to frighten them. If you can figure out a way to scare people, you can make them do what you want.'

And the German people certainly bought into fear!

And what about the more recent Iraq War? Tony Blair and his buddy George Bush declaring that Iraq had nuclear weapons and needed to be attacked. Pushing the agenda of fear, - in this case fear of terrorism! And this, despite the fact that no weapons were ever found! Sure the entire world knows it was the oil they were after from the very start, - *'It's the economy, stupid!'*

And the current war in Ukraine? How many more years before we know the truth about what started this conflict? What lies are we being told about this? What truths are being kept from us? What are the particular government agendas at work here? But there is one thing we can know for sure! All will be revealed in time! Simply because there is **nothing hidden that will not be revealed!**

And what about how the wars against the Native Americans were portrayed? The cowboys and Indians films! The Native Americans always the baddies, the white men always the heroes! But we now know the truth! All those false portrayals just a cover-up for plunder, pillage and murder! And President Obama apologising for the wrongs committed against the Native Americans and other indigenous peoples? He would hardly have apologised if it had all never actually happened! Proof indeed that it did! And not a so-called 'conspiracy theory'!

We have been taught that the conquistadores of the Americas were adventurers, explorers, heroes, in the ongoing search for new lands. And very little about the competition between Spain and Portugal for dominance and wealth, through finding new trade routes to the exotic treasures of the East. Treasures to be plundered and stolen!

We have been taught that in that competition between Portugal and Spain, Christopher Columbus sailed westward from Spain across the Atlantic Ocean on a mission to find a new trade route to the east, to Asia, - for Spain. Remember learning that? And how those 'Voyages of Discovery' as they were called in the history books were all depicted as adventurous and exciting, and of course, bringing civilisation to those savage peoples, bringing Christianity!

But the truth? In 1492, when Columbus first reached the Americas, - present day Bahamas, - he encountered the peaceful Lucayan people of the region, immediately becoming obsessed with the gold jewellery they wore around their necks, and forced them into leading his party to where their gold deposits could be found. Over the course of several years, Columbus returned many times to Cuba and Hispaniola, and each time he returned home again to Spain, he brought with him great numbers of slaves and large amounts of the gold.

Gold! The ultimate find! Gold! The most expensive of metals!

Gold is soft, dense, malleable, ductile and conducts electricity well. It is resistant, in that it does not tarnish, crumble, discolour, or get affected by most solvents. It helps reduce heat and glare from sunlight, reflecting infrared light. Astronauts' spacesuits are lined with a thin layer of gold, including their visors, as they are at danger from ultraviolet rays and space radiation. One astronaut suit alone costs $120 million! And gold is used today in virtually all of our electronics including computers and cell phones.

And so it was that the Spanish Empire turned their sights on the Caribbean! So it was that the gold mining in the Caribbean was done through forced labour, by the native people, through back-breaking and brutal working conditions. There is no record of the countless numbers of indigenous workers who died in the process. And what about all the diseases the Spanish brought to these indigenous peoples! We do not read about any of this in our history books! Or how Columbus raided and plundered the native gold reserves! Why are we not taught all of this at school?- Because, of course, history is written by the winners! And the winners always need to justify their actions!

Then in 1519, Herman Cortes landed on the eastern shores of Mexico, near the present-day town of Veracruz. Then he and his men moved inland towards the capital city of Tenochtitlan, the land of the Aztecs, levelling the city to the ground. The Aztecs were massacred in their thousands. The modern-day Mexico City was then built over the ashes of Tenochtitlan, all under the approving and watchful eye of none other than the Catholic Church.

Further invasions followed, all in the pursuit of gold. The Incas of Peru met the same fate as the Aztecs, in 1532, under Francisco Pizarro who landed on the coast of Ecuador, and was soon joined with reinforcements by Hernando De Soto.

The Spanish conquest of the Americas claimed the lives of hundreds of thousands of indigenous people and led to the collapse of the Hopi and Puebloan cultures of Southwest United States, the Aztec and Maya of Mexico, and the Inca of South America. Civilisations all completely wiped out! Their resources and artifacts plundered, pillaged and stolen, many of their sacred texts later taken to Rome where they were locked and sealed for secrecy under the Vatican, in huge underground vaults.

Have you ever wondered from where the Vatican got its vast wealth? All those priceless art works! All those countless artifacts! All those valuable ancient texts! And the Vatican connection with Nazi Germany? Where did all the Nazi priceless artwork disappear to? How come the history books do not tell us about that?

And likewise, have you ever wondered how monarchs and the institutions of monarchy accumulated most of their wealth and privilege? And the answer? - On the backs of indigenous peoples! Slavery! Exploitation! Conquests! How come that is not in our history books?

And how many of us were ever taught anything about the infamous *'Document of Discovery'*? The *'Decree of Discovery'* that still exists! The same *'Decree of Discovery'* that has never been revoked! The same *'Decree of Discovery'* that still to this day and in this day and age, sanctions and promotes the conquest, colonisation and exploitation of non-Christian territories and peoples worldwide! The 'Doctrine of Discovery' that allows for laws that invalidate or ignore indigenous people's rights, sovereignty and humanity in Canada, the United States, Australia and across the globe! A principle of international law that was created by Pope Nicholas V in 1452. Through the issue of a Papal Bull, the Portuguese Empire could now conquer and enslave 'pagans' - and all with the Church's blessing.

And so it was that in 1493, the year after the arrival of that first Spanish-sponsored expedition to the Americas, Pope Alexander VI, well known for his corruption, issued the papal bull 'Inter Caetera'. Any land not inhabited by Christians could now be claimed and 'barbarous nations be overthrown and brought to the faith itself.' And this allowed the Spanish, Portuguese, French and British Empires to devour more of Africa and the Americas. Not forgetting that the struggle and competition for colonies between these same empires, especially in Africa, was one of the major reasons for World War One.

And so humanity has a long tradition of horrendous acts all done in the 'name of God'. But these papal bulls just mentioned were simply a continuation of what had been going on since at least the 8th century, from Charlemagne, through the Crusades, then the Inquisition, the war on witches, the Reconquista of the Iberian Peninsula. And all over indigenous rights and sovereignty.

And those decrees are still with us today! They have never yet been revoked! Even when the late Queen Elizabeth II of England was asked to rescind the 'Doctrine of Discovery', she failed to act! So it is all up to King Charles now! What is he going to do about the rights of indigenous peoples? Keeping in mind how monarchs have accumulated most of their wealth!

And here in our own country! The lies that we have been told, - and taught! The 1845 Famine, for example! That has been explained in the history books as having been caused by the potato blight, an act of God, a weather phenomenon! Nobody's fault! No mention of the fact that the same blight hit England and America, - with little or no effect! No mention of the fact that Ireland was totally dependent on the potato for survival because of the system of absentee landlords, subdivision of holdings, high rents and frequent evictions. And no mention of the fact that while the Irish people died from starvation, large amounts of grain were being shipped out of the country!

And the 1800 Act of Union! The Act passed by the British Government under the Prime Minister William Pitt the Younger! The Act of Parliament that joined Ireland onto England! We have been led to believe that the Irish protestants voted for this, and the Irish Catholics against it! In fact, it was the opposite! Irish protestants voted against it because they held all the power in the Dublin Government and stood to lose that power in a united Great Britain. And the catholics voted for it, simply because Pitt promised them Catholic Emancipation in return, - which, needless to say, never materialised. Another clear example of how any and every promise is made to ensure a successful government agenda outcome! And then broken! That's how governments work! Tell people what they want to hear, buy into them, promise them anything! And the campaign of killing, bribery and corruption that resulted in the 1800 Act of Union? Lord Castlereagh was the British government official in charge, -

'I met murder on the way / He wore a mask like Castlereagh.'

What a way to go down in history! What a way to be remembered!

The campaign of fear! The campaign of fear rolled out by governments to ensure compliance! We saw it all during the recent pandemic. Scare-mongering! Psychological and emotional black-mailing! The World War One slogans '*Your country needs you*' simply replaced with '*The NHS needs you*', and the 'Join *up and save lives*' replaced with '*Stay at home, save lives*'. The words '*need*' *and* '*save*' being two of the most emotive words in the English language!

Responsibility for our own lives and our own health was stealthily taken from us over the last few years. We handed that over! We fell into the trap! We swallowed the bait!

And another fact that is sad but true? It was all based on estimates! Or, as '*they*' term it in posh talk, in euphemisms, - '*extrapolations*'. And of course, not to even mention '*algorithms*'!

So, as can see, it's all about conditioning! And as Goebbels said: '*The truth is the greatest enemy of the state!*'

And when the truth becomes the greatest enemy, - then we are in serious trouble! Time to WAKE UP!

And we must not forget what we have always been taught about ancient Egypt, the pharaohs and the pyramids!

The pyramids of Giza, just outside Cairo! Built by the pharaohs as burial tombs! Built by millions of slaves hauling massive slabs of concrete up on pulleys over their shoulders! Remember learning all that?

BUT! How come even to this day, not as much as even one dead or alive pharaoh has been found inside any pyramid, anywhere! That's because they are not there! And they were never there! Even when any sarcophagus was found there were no human remains inside! The pharaohs were all buried in the south of Egypt, over 400 miles from Giza, in the famous Valley of the Kings. During Egypt's New Kingdom (1539-1075 B.C.), the Valley of the Kings became a royal burial ground for pharaohs such as Tutankhamun, Seti I, and Ramses II, as well as queens, high priests, and other elites of the 18th, 19th, and 20th dynasties. All mummified and buried in the Valley of the Kings! And NOT in the pyramids! - More lies!

So what were the pyramids really used for? Why were they really built? And why have we been continuously lied to about this? Remember George Orwell's words? - 'Who controls the past controls the future. Who controls the present controls the past.'

Yes! - It's all about control!

Not only are the pyramids of Giza far older than we have been taught, but they were NOT actually built by the pharaohs at all! Evidence now shows that these pyramids were constructed by a lost civilisation who disappeared from this earth during the time of the last great ice age.

AND! The Great Pyramid and the Sphinx at Giza perfectly reflect and are perfectly aligned to the star constellations of Orion's Belt, Leo and Canis Major, and were all constructed about 13,000 years ago! And the water erosion marks found along the edges of the Sphinx further testify to the fact that these constructions are far older than we have been taught! And the Temple of Seti in the Egyptian city of Abydos, believed to have been built around 1300 BC by pharaoh Seti 1, and also known as the Great Temple of Abydos, is notable for its Abydos graffiti, ancient Phoenician and Aramaic graffiti found on the temple walls. The long list of the pharaohs of the principal dynasties—recognized by Seti—are carved on a wall and known as the 'Abydos King List'. The eroded hieroglyphs, though now retouched, are said to represent modern vehicles – a helicopter, a submarine, and a zeppelin or plane.

It is becoming more and more apparent now that the pyramids were built as some sort of electricity or thermal energy generator or harmonic fertilising machine. Easy to believe when we remember that the ancient Egyptians were wizards of engineering. Yes, the pyramids are all about energy! And the creation of energetic spheres. All built on the natural energy lines, the ley lines of the earth. The place of a convergence of strong energy centers! That's the reason why the pyramids were built in that particular place! To utilise and harness the abundant electromagnetic energy that is there!

And the Bosnian pyramid right in the centre of Bosnia! It is now believed that this pyramid, like all the others, is a healing energy facilitator, and a regeneration processor. The powerful energy of the pyramid is so beneficial in the healing process.

And megalithic structures and monuments are not just found in Egypt, but all over the world. And here in Ireland we have Loughcrew and Newgrange, along with countless others. All bearing testimony to the fact that a sophisticated society was alive and thriving many centuries ago longer than we have been led to believe.

And Plato, in his writings, known as the 'Timae and Critias', writing about the lost sophisticated civilisation of Atlantis! All corroborated in the Mesopotamian cuneiform tablets and Biblical writings. Yet all of this never given credence in our education systems!

But why? Simply because if we were to awaken to the fact that humanity and life on this planet is much much older than we have been led to believe, and if we were to awaken to the fact that ancient civilisations were NOT primitive, but highly advanced and sophisticated, with technology we can hardly even imagine, and if we were to awaken to the fact that ancient civilisations were on a much higher level of *'consciousness'*, a higher level of *'awareness'* than we are today, - then that would spell disaster for the Elite of this world who are controlling us through they themselves writing the narrative of the history of humanity!

Knowledge is power! I am emphasising this yet again! And by depriving us and denying us the knowledge of all this, - the knowledge of how we should perceive our evolution, our human origins and our purpose in the universe and our place in the multiverse and the entirety of all creation, - then we are much more easily controlled! Deprived of this knowledge of our inter-cosmic connections, those who rule and are depriving us of this knowledge, - they are currently big fish in a small one-world pond when they allow us to see ourselves only as this earth, but in a huge cosmic pond, they would be very small fish indeed! They are fighting for their own very survival!

Time to WAKE UP!

And of course, it is not just history, governments and politicians who have lied to us! We have been lied to and deceived by Church leaders and controlling religions. God is NOT how we have been led to believe. Again, we have bought into a particular belief system because of fear! And guilt! Fear and Guilt! - A debilitating, paralysing, suffocating combination!

Fear of eternal damnation by a judgemental, punishing, despotic, vengeful God! Fear of hell! Fire and brimstone! For all eternity! No way out! No reprieve! No second chance! You blew it! - Tough!

Any religious belief system that relies on instilling fear and guilt, any religious belief system that takes away man's own inherent ability to connect with all things spiritual; any religious belief system that denies the natural essence of man; any religious belief system that murders and kills millions of people who do not agree with that belief system and who do not obey its laws; any religious belief system founded on manmade laws and doctrines of punishment, lies and misinformation; any religious belief system which has vast amounts of material wealth while so many people in the world have nothing; any religious belief system based on theatrical spectacle and drama; any religious belief system that sets itself up as the only way to God; any religious belief system which abuses young children and harbours and protects the abusers; any religious belief system that promotes God as a male figure, at the expense of the feminine; any religious belief system that teaches that the natural sexual act is sinful and disgraceful; any religious belief system that controls and invades every aspect of one's life; any religious belief system that continues to be rigid and uncompromising with regards to divorce, separation, etc., - how can any of these be for the good of humanity?

And how have most of us experienced religion? Does our personal experience support or contradict any of the above? I can only speak for myself! And for me, religion when I was younger was not about love, but about fear, - fear of punishment. And of course, guilt! As we have seen previously, the two most lethal and mighty weapons in any arsenal!

Religion is simply a belief system. A believe system that we have bought into! But to '*just believe*' to just '*have faith',* as religion dictates, does not equal truth or fact! And religion can never solve the problems of the world. Religion can never unite us, - simply because religion by its very nature, is divisive, deceitful, and manipulating. But yet we continue to blindly obey! Remember the words of Oscar Wilde, quoted earlier? -

'Disobedience, in the eyes of any one who has read history, is man's original virtue.'

In actual fact, can any one of us deny that buying into religion is simply buying into fear and guilt? When we buy into any controlled religion, we are singing someone else's song! Our soul is not singing its own song, as it is meant to sing, free from fear and guilt, - to sound its own unique note in the glorious harmony of the one great universal orchestra, flying freely, unfettered by the chains and ropes of dictating, controlling, man-made religious dogmas and doctrines.

And what about all those stories we have bought into through controlling religion?

Just as in all those fairy tales, where there was no Goldilocks, no Cinderella, no Little Red Riding, so too, in the stories in the canonical gospels, we are not reading about the life of a man called Jesus, the Son of God who died on the cross to save humanity.

Yes, there may well have been a man called Jesus teaching in Palestine at the time of the supposed life of Jesus in the gospels, but ***it is not the story of that man's life that is being told to us in those gospels***! The Jesus we read about in the canonical gospels is merely a re-hash, a re-make of the same mythological gods permeating history for thousands of years before the invention of Christianity. Jesus is simply the last, the most recent in a long line of such gods, - Jesus, the god of Christianity!

They all share the same C.V.! The same C.V. - **'A God's Life'!**

And who were these gods? Let's put some names on them! Let's identify them!

In India, for example, there was Krishna, born in 900 B.C.E. and Buddha; in Egypt there was Re or Ra, then Horus, born 3000 B.C.E. and Osiris; and in Greece, - Apollo. Then in Persia there was Mithra born 1200 B.C.E; in Arabia there was Isa; in Greece, Dionysus, born 500 B.C.E; in Phrygia, Attis born 1200 B.C.E; in Sumeria, Tammuz, born 2600 B.C.E; in Egypt, Serapis, Adonis, Aesclepius, Heracles, Zeus; in Assyria, Adad and Marduk; in Scandinavia, Odin; in Crete, Chaldea; in Afghanistan, Bali; in Mexico, Quetzalcoatl; in Japan, Beddun; in China, Tien; in Syria, Adad; in Thebes, Alcides; in Rome, Jupiter, Quirinius, Neptune, Venus, Mars; for the Druids and the Gauls there were Hesus, Thor, Lugh, Dann. Dagda; for the Sintoos there was Mikado. The list goes on!

And for Christianity it was Jesus! Full name given, - Jesus Christ. And all these gods were long before the supposed time of Jesus! And all these gods share the same life details! Yes, all of them were:

- Born on 25th December, at the winter solstice, born of a virgin, in a manger or stable

- Of royal descent

- Birth was heralded by a cosmic event, such as a bright star in the east and visited by three wise men

- Taught in the temple at an early age

- Had twelve companions or disciples

- Performed various miracles, such as walking on water, turning water into wine, raising people from the dead, exorcising demons

- Died for humanity, dead for 3 days, and then rose again

And I have detailed the lives of each of these gods in a few previous books: - *'Out of the Darkness of Deception and Despair into the Light of Truth'* ; and *'The Almost Immaculate Deception! - The Greatest Scam in History?'*

And of course, we have the iconic image in Christianity of the Virgin Mary with the Christ child in her arms! But the image of Isis, the Egyptian mother of Horus, with her son in her arms was well known around all the Mediterranean countries since the fourth century B.C.E. long before the supposed time of Jesus!

And all the similarities in the teachings of Buddha and the teachings of Jesus!

And again, I have covered all of this in a previous book, *'The Truth will set you free.....Christianity, where did it all begin?'*

Yes! The story of Christianity is neither original nor unique! It is NOT as we have been led to believe! It is in fact based in the stars! In the common ancient astrotheological and astromythological story of the **Sun** of God!

As Thomas Paine wrote:

'The Christian religion is a parody on the worship of the Sun, in which they put a man whom they call Christ, in the place of the Sun, and pay him the same adoration which was originally paid to the Sun.'

First of all, the birth sequence and life-story of all of these gods is completely astrological. **'Sirius'** is the brighest star in the night sky. On December 24th every year, around the time of the winter solstice, Sirius aligns with the three brightest stars in Orion's Belt. And those three stars are still known today as they were known to the ancients, long before the first century C.E.

And the name of those three stars? **'The Three Kings'**! Or **'Magi'**! And those three brightest stars and Sirius all point to the place of the sunrise on 25th December, the place where the sun rises, the place where the **'Sun of God'** rises. The three stars look towards the star in the East, - Sirius, in order to locate the sunrise, the *'birth of God's Sun',* the birth of the sun after the winter solstice. So hence the three wise men following the star to find Jesus! The *'sun (son) of God'*! And hence 25th December being designated as the birthday of all the ancient gods!

The winter solstice represented to the ancients the demise of the sun, and was a symbol of death. The word *'solstice'* (sol-stice) itself means *'sun standing still'*. On 22nd December, the sun sinks to its lowest point in the sky and remains still, or at least was perceived to remain still for three days. On 25th December, it begins to rise and move north again, symbolising the bringing of longer days, warmth and spring. The transition period of the sun, before it moves again into the northern hemisphere is three days.

Three days! The length of time Jesus, and all the other gods before him were dead before their resurrection! And during those three days that the sun was perceived to be still, it remained firmly in the southern hemisphere, in the vicinity of the star constellation **'The Southern *Cross'*** or the **'Crux'**. Then the sun *'rises'* again on the third day.

So! ***The Sun of God died on the Cross, was dead for three days and then came again!***

It cannot be more clear!

Here is the source of the '***greatest story ever told***' or indeed the '***greatest story never told',*** or even the '***greatest story ever sold',*** which most people think refers to the story of the life of Jesus in the canonical gospels. And yes, in a way it does, as the life of Jesus as in the canonical gospels replicates this astrological story, this ***astromythological*** story. But the life of Jesus is not the original story! The original '***greatest story ever told '*** is the story of the '***Sun of God***' in its journey through its yearly cycle of birth, death and resurrection, as was perceived by the ancients in the astrological movements of the heavenly bodies, and explained by them through the personification of the planets and stars.

And so the story of Jesus as in the canonical gospels is astrological and astrotheological, non-historical, based on a mythical character, the result of thousands of years of observation by the ancients of the movements and inter-relationships of the stars and planets.

There may well have been a man called Jesus, travelling somewhere around Galilee or Judaea, healing and teaching. But! It is not the story of that Jesus that is being told in the gospels! Those gospels are giving us a rehash, a clear and obvious regurgitation of the same old myth that has been trundling down through history from ancient times! There has just been a change of name!

There is nothing original, unique, or new in the four canonical gospels!

For example, in the Egyptian **'Pyramid Texts',** dating from the third millennium B.C.E we read in the '*Beloved Son'* script, the Sky Goddess

Nut, speaking from heaven regarding the deceased, who becomes Osiris, remarking:

'...*This is my son, my first born.... this is my beloved, with whom I have been satisfied!*'

Compare this with Matthew 3:17, and the voice from heaven at the baptism of Jesus, '*This is my beloved son with whom I am well pleased*'.

And also from Mark:

'*You are my own dear Son. I am pleased with you*'. (Mark 1:11)

And at the transfiguration of Jesus, a voice is heard, again coming from heaven:

'*This is my own dear Son, with whom I am pleased - listen to him!*' (Matthew 17:5)

So we can see there is a lot of plagiarism going on! Plagiarism in particular of the Egyptian Sun God Horus! In the Temple of Luxor, there for all to see, dating from several thousand years before the supposed time of Jesus, paintings and carvings on the walls clearly depict the story of the god Thoth announcing the news to Isis that she is to be the virgin mother of Horus, an event obviously plagiarised in the feast of the Annunciation of the Christian Church, the day the Archangel Gabriel announced to the virgin Mary that she was to bear a son, a saviour god. The virgin Isis is impregnated by Neth, - the '*Holy Ghost*' of the conception of Jesus, - and the child in each case is adored by three kings. Further scenes depict the suffering and death of Horus on the cross, and then his resurrection three days afterwards.

And all this was drawn on the walls of the Luxor Temple in Egypt thousands of years before Jesus was supposedly born!

So everything would appear to point to the conclusion that Jesus *as in the canonical gospels* never existed! And we need to remember, no historian of that time gives us any details about Jesus! Here we have this man-god working the most amazing miracles, raising people from the dead, walking on water and all the other wonderous feats, and the historians of the time do not tell us about him! So what conclusion can we come to from this? **Not one historian tells us about the amazing miracles of this man called Jesus!**

And that is obviously because the person we have been taught was Jesus, the supernatural god-man, the saviour-god, born of a virgin on 25th December, who was crucified and died on the cross for all mankind, then resurrected three days later, was simply myth dressed up as history.

The only place we hear about a figure called Jesus, performing all these miracles, is in the four canonical gospels of the Roman Christian Church, the gospels of Matthew, Mark, Luke and John. Gospels which have been shown to be totally unreliable as historical writings, re-edited time and time again, full of historical inaccuracies, geographical inaccuracies, contradictions, discrepancies and copying! Gospels which belong in the field of mythological literature, and not in the field of history. And gospels which were clearly written specifically as Roman propaganda! Gospels and New Testament writings full of instructions to the rebellious Jewish people to *'pay your taxes to Caesar'; 'Love those who persecute you'; 'turn the other cheek'; 'obey your rulers, they are sent by God'; 'slaves, obey your masters'.*

And the only later references we have to Jesus are from Christian

Church apologists! Those early Roman Christian Church defenders! Those early Roman Christian Church fathers intent on bolstering up their creation! Eusebius, early fourth-century Church father and writer! Regarded by most modern scholars as the liar-for-God! Eusebius, regarded by most modern scholars as the person responsible for the interpolation, the '**Testimonium Flavianum**', that short paragraph later inserted into the works of the first-century Jewish historian Josephus about Jesus! An interpolation which no Church apologist before Eusebius mentions, and why not? Simply because it was not in the original works of Josephus, but inserted by Eusebius in 340 C.E. as trumped-up evidence for the historical life of Jesus.

Eusebius himself, in his '*Evangelical Demonstration*' wrote:

'*Certainly the attestations I have already produced concerning our Saviour may be sufficient. However, it may not be amiss, if, over and above, we make use of Josephus the Jew for a further witness*'. (Eusebius, '*Evangelical Demonstration*', Book iii, page 124)

And again, in his own words,

'.....*it is necessary sometimes to use falsehoods as a medicine for those who need such an approach*'.

Eusebius, well known to most scholars as one who advocated, and did himself, re-edit, interpolate and pervert texts in order to fulfil what he regarded as the just task of getting the early Roman Christian Church established!

And of course, how can we forget the words of Pope Leo X in 1514, as recorded by his secretary, Pietro Cardinal Bembo:

'How well we know what a profitable superstition this false fable of Christ has been for us and our predecessors'.

There it is! Right from the very highest of the Roman Christian Church hierarchy! From the mouth of Pope Leo himself!

And our understanding of the four canonical gospels? The four canonical gospels on which Christianty is founded? Again, I have dealt with how gravely we have been misled in all of this in a previous book *'And that's the Gospel truth!'*

The gospels were NOT written by the disciples of Jesus. They are NOT four independent sources. They were written first in Greek, and by very highly literate people, almost a century after the supposed death of the supposed Jesus, and they were NOT written by authors who were familiar with the territory of the Jewish people, as they are full of geographical inaccuracies, for example place-names such as *'Nazareth'* which most scholars now agree did not exist at that time, and which is not mentioned by the first century Jewish historian Josephus, who himself hailed from that very same area and knew it intimately! And of course, no hint at all in the canonical gospels of the violent and dangerous territory in which Jesus was travelling and teaching! A boiling hot-pot of rebellion, a simmering cauldron of Jewish hatred and resentment against Roman occupation! Definitely NOT the image with which we have been presented, of a peaceful land and Jesus casually wandering around strutting his stuff! And with his twelve disciples in tow!

And when we consider all of this, is it not indeed truly ironic that the Roman Catholic Church continues to vilify astrology and strongly discourages its members from partaking in any form of star-gazing, looking to the stars, reading horoscopes, or the use of astronomy in any way for fortune telling or other practices based on movements of the celestial bodies in the heavens? That very same Church that owes its own origins to that same study of astrology and astronomy! That very same Church that condemned and persecuted such men as Copernicus and Galileo for daring to contradict Church teachings by showing that the earth revolves around the sun, instead of the sun revolving around the earth, as the Church had taught! Such new discoveries, even though they were proven to be true, threatened the authority of the Church establishment, that same Church establishment that stubbornly insisted on teaching that the world was the epicenter of the visible universe, and anyone who dared to question or contradict their stance was condemned as a heretic and subjected to the most cruel of tortures. One such person was Giordano Bruno, 1548-1600, an Italian monk, who went further than Copernicus in suggesting that stars were suns with planets orbiting around them, and they were inhabited by other beings:

'There are innumerable suns and an infinite number of planets which circle around their suns in a manner similar to the way the seven planets revolve around our sun .... innumerable suns exist. Living beings inhabit these worlds.' (Bruno, 'De l'infinito universo e mundi', 26-28)

Bruno, just like many before and after him, paid the ultimate price for his theories. He was arrested by the papal Inquisition and tortured, but refused to recant. He was sentenced to be publicly burned alive, and his statue now marks the spot in Campo de Fiori, Rome, where the horrific and gorey event was witnessed. An entry in the Vatican's records for 17th February 1600 reads:

'Giordano Bruno was led by officers of the law to Campo de' Fiori, and there, stripped naked and tied to the stake, he was burned alive, always

accompanied by our company singing the litanies, and the comforters, up to the last, urging him to abandon his obstinacy, with which he ended his miserable and unhappy life.' (Quoted from *'Cosmic Womb'*, Chandra Wickramasinghe and Robert Bauval)

And in 1930, who was declared a saint by Pope Pius XI? None other than the chief inquisitor at Bruno's trial, Cardinal Roberto Bellarmino!

Even to this day, castigated and condemned as the work of the devil, which itself is of course another Christian invention meant to instil fear and terror in us, there is still a deliberate attempt on the part of the Roman Christian Church to prevent people from finding the astrological imagery permeating the Christian Bible, hence keeping people in ignorance and so in subjugation. All those people who still believe the gospels to be the inspired word of God and take them all literally, are simply failing to recognise that the gospels are composed of allegories and symbolism, and are not true stories. Allegories and symbolism based on the movements of the planets and stars and their connection and inter-relationships with each other, and with us here on Planet Earth.

And we must not forget Leonardo da Vinci! Genius of the Medieval Renaissance! Leonardo da Vinci who has hidden so many clues in his paintings for us to find! Information that he had to conceal, unable to speak out openly for fear of terrible reprisal from the Roman Christian Church! Leonardo da Vinci who had no time for Jesus and the holy family! The same holy family held up to us as the model family! God the Father sitting on his throne in heaven, on his right side the virgin mother, and on his other side, the celibate son! A model family? More like a dysfunctional family! Leonardo da Vinci certainly knew more than he could say openly or write! Da Vinci's paintings have been admired and seen as masterpieces since the Middle Ages, but we need to start *really looking* at them! We need to *really look* and see the coded hidden messages within them! The painting of the *'Last Supper',* for example, with Mary Magdalene at the side of Jesus, and all that male anger of the disciples directed towards her. Or the painting of the *'Mona Lisa'!* Or the painting of *'John the Baptist'* with a defiant and dismissive first finger pointing upwards! All sending coded and hidden messages to us! Leonardo da Vinci was indeed just following the normal ancient system of coding and hiding layers of meanings beneath the surface words and brush strokes!

But that was then, this is now. And today, we have lost the ability to accomplish this particular skill. We live in a world of computers and highly advanced technology where the human brain is not required to work as it did for our ancestors in previous centuries.

But we just must face the facts! Astrological symbols and motifs are found in every Christian Church. Yes, the Christian Church is full of pagan symbols and sayings, clearly seen in the Vatican and in all Christian rituals and ceremonies. And remember too, as we saw earlier, Christianity castigated the pagans as heathens and undesirables, but at the same time took over from them their ceremonial sites, which were built on the natural energy lines of the earth, and then proceeded to build their own churches on the same sites. The Vatican itself is built above the remains of a temple complex dedicated to Mithra, a god widely revered by Roman soldiers. And most Christian churches face eastwards, the place where the *'Sun of God'* rises!

So we just have to face the facts here! The facts being that there is nothing new in Christianity! And there is nothing new in the symbols evident in all Christian churches and in the Vatican!

The Vatican is built over the remains of a ceremonial complex devoted to Mithra, and the writings of Paul, formerly Saul of Tarsus, on which much of the Roman Christian teachings are founded, reflect strongly the beliefs of Mithraism. Almost all of the elements of the Roman Catholic Church rituals and ceremonies are taken directly from earlier pagan religions such as Mithraism, and can be clearly seen in the Vatican and in all Catholic churches. Roman Christian Church doctrines such as infant baptism with the sprinkling of holy water, celibate priests, prayers to the dead and to relics, repetitive prayers with the use of beads, doctrines on the forgiveness of sins, teachings on hell and a punishing God, the mass, Sunday worship, are all derived from ancient Babylon, not the so-called Christian bible!

So, to summarise! The stories surrounding the lives of all of the gods of the ancient civilisations are remarkably similar. Going back 7000 years before the supposed time of Jesus in the canonical gospels, we have a long line of gods permeating and running down through history, from Horus, Krishna, Attis, Mithra, Dionysus, and all the others we have just mentioned. Each personifying the '***Sun of God'***, each just given a different name, and the story of one life is the same story for every life. And that common story is the story of the sun as it was perceived in its yearly journey through the twelve signs of the zodiac.

All of these stories and all of these gods belong firmly in the field of mythology, in the field of mythological literature, in the field of mythicism, and not in the field of history.

And let us remind ourselves of the nature of myths and mythicism. Myths are simply made-up stories, incorporating made-up happenings and made-up characters for the purpose of getting across a particular message, a particular lesson, a particular moral. Those characters did not exist in real life!

And the last in the line, the most recent of these gods was the god of Christianity, none other than Jesus Christ. And the story of Jesus Christ, the god of Christianity, like the story of the lives of all the other gods, is all in the stars!

The ancient civilisations created the myths and legends of the gods, based on thousands of years of studying the planets and stars and their relationships to each other. We today consider those ancient myths to be just stories. But to the ancients, as we have seen, they were much more than just stories! Mythological writing was one of the highest arts and one of the highest acclaimed skills in ancient times, myths being a source not only of entertainment, but more importantly a source through which spiritual teachings were transmitted, and on various levels within the one story, so each person took from them only what they were ready to hear and accept. A bit like George Orwell's 'Animal Farm', in our own time. 'Animal Farm' can be enjoyed on the surface level, the animals all playing their part in getting rid of Mr. Jones and setting up their own farm, working just for themselves, all meant to be equal, but where it turns out some are 'more equal than others'. Reading at the deeper level though, the novel is actually about the Communist Revolution in Russia in 1917, with every animal representing a particular person in that Communist Revolution, and every event representing an event that actually happened during the Revolution. But if you do not actually know about this aspect to it, you can still enjoy the story.

Just like Jesus and his parables! Stories where there were several layers of meaning, each person taking from them according to his own state of readiness at any one particular time. Remember what you read in a previous chapter about us all being at a different level of consciousness? At a different level of awareness? And hence we all get a different level of meaning out of what we read, - the level we are able to absorb at any given time, depending on our own individual level of awareness.

So, in ancient times, there was a hierarchy of meaning, a hierarchy of esoteric teachings being delivered through each myth. Those god figures, through which ancient civilisations personified the planets and stars, were central to their lives, simply because in the life-stories they built around their gods, they understood life, death and re-birth in an on-going cycle, each god the hero in his own life-story, each god, through his life experiences, through facing his life challenges, overcoming his own darker nature, and reaching immortality by transcending physical death. And there is only the one story, the story of the rise of the hero within each of us. And the ancient gods were no different!

Mythology and astrotheology were real concerns and matters of importance to ancient civilisations, as the planets, stars and the celestial bodies guided them to make sense of the universe around them, indicating when the Nile would flood, for example, which meant their irrigation system for their crops, and guiding them through the main events of their lives on a yearly cyclical basis. The New Testament writings, no less than the writings of the ancient civilisations, were composed of spiritual allegories, all with the purpose of teaching the harmonic nature of the entirety of creation, all providing deep spiritual insights into the mysteries of the Ancient Mystery Schools, teachings all handed down orally for thousands of years before being recorded in writing.

So the origins of Christianity? It's literally all in the stars! And NOT in the Christian bible or the canonical gospels!

So history has not told us the truth! Governments and politicians have not been telling us the truth! Churches and religions have not been telling us the truth!

Anyone else?

Oh yes! - Mainstream media!

The 'news' and 'information' delivered to us through mainstream media, - it's all propaganda! Brain washing! Spin! Biased reporting! Fake news! And all with a particular agenda in mind! Social engineering, social manipulation!

And so it is indeed ironic that the most stifling, the most suffocating, the most covert and dictatorial operation in the history of the media was called '*Operation Mockingbird'!* Ironic indeed, because the mockingbird is the power animal symbol for overcoming fear, the symbol of speaking your truth, the word '*Mockingbird*' itself meaning '*many tongued mimic*'. This is one of the few birds that sings whilst flying. In other words, it is never quiet! And Operation Mockingbird proves that the press is corrupt to its very core.

When I was growing up in the 1960s, the daily newspapers, and then in particular, the Sunday newspapers were all part of one's day. As was the daily news on radio and then television. Not to be missed! This was where you found out what was going on in the world. You trusted that what you were reading, what you were hearing, what you were seeing, was the truth. If you read it in the papers or heard it on the radio or saw it on television, then it had to be true!

Before the birth of the internet, and along with it Facebook, Twitter and the like, a handful of people had control over information being pumped out to us through the four or so channels on television. That was then, but this is now. And how things have changed! Not changed for the media, but changed for us! Now, today, with thousands of platforms, we thought that would end this control. But it has had the exact opposite result, - what we are seeing still is the control of many, many platforms, by a handful of major private social networks.

We can no longer believe anything, never mind everything that we read, hear or see in the mainstream media. And why not? Because censorship has become rampant, pervasive, becoming the norm rather than the exception. If you have NOT been de-platformed by some form of social media, then it makes people wonder why. What have you NOT been saying? Why have you NOT been censored?

So if you want to know what is going on in the world, do not watch or listen to the news programmes! And do not read the newspapers! It's all fake news!

And here in Ireland, we witnessed that fake news first-hand when Pope Francis came to the country in August 2018. All the photographs that were put out on the media were carefully managed to show crowds everywhere! But there were no crowds at any one place, never mind everywhere! I remember watching it, out of curiosity, just to see how they would fiddle and manipulate everything, and sure enough, there in Nassau Street, in the middle of Dublin, was one of RTE's best-known female presenters and reporters, on a platform, talking to two teenagers about the excitement of the Pope's visit, and commenting on how the crowd was so big behind her! But Nassau Street behind her was empty! And the same in Phoenix Park! The camera very carefully homed in on the spots where people had gathered, but beyond that, there were vast huge empty spaces! We even saw some young boys running alongside the Pope's transport vehicle, waving at him and screaming! I wonder how much they got paid for their contribution? And if they were able to run freely alongside the Pope, then there must not have been any great numbers of people in their way! And there wasn't!

Again, let me draw you back to the scenes splashed across our television screens on all channels a few years ago, of the countless immigrants and refugees trekking across Europe for weeks on end, seeking sanctuary. There they were, babies in arms, old people being carried, walking for up to 45 miles per day. BUT! Some of them were wearing flip-flops! Walking 45 miles per day in flip-flops? And where was their luggage? Where were the nappies for the babies? Where was their food? There was none! And why not? Because it was all staged! All propaganda! Those people were paid to put on a show! Transported to the scene in bus loads! As a recent disclosure documentary showed! And television can do wonders with the use of mirrors to increase numbers!

And then on another occasion there was the photo shot of a young girl being pulled from the wreckage of a bombed building. But the same girl turned up time and time again being pulled from bombed buildings in other places as well! I wonder how much she got paid for her efforts?

David Sedgwick is an author, journalist and university lecturer specialising in Linguistics and Cultural Studies. In his book, 'The Fake

News Factory', Sedgwick gives the example of how, after an April 2018 chemical attack in Douma in Syria, BBC news reports of the incident were extremely harrowing, showing child victims at a hospital being urgently doused in water aided by oxygen masks. This was just the latest atrocity committed by Assad's regime, or so the BBC told us.

Or was it? News reports appeared to show an 11-year old boy Hassan Diab being doused in water by frantic medics upon arrival at Douma hospital, a victim of the alleged *'gas attack'.*

'Tracked down by reporter Evgeniy Poddubnyy the 'victim' told a very different story. Lured to the hospital by promises of food, on arrival he had been grabbed by persons unknown and much to his surprise doused in water. According to the boy's father many children were given dates and biscuits before being sent home - rewarded presumably for their participation in the 'film'. Hassan's story stacked up. Footage clearly shows him, along with other children being doused with water amid scenes of panic.' (David Sedgwick, *'The Fake News Factory'* page 148)

So you see, it's all propaganda! All lies! All fake news! All with a specific agenda in mind!

William Casey, Director of Central Intelligence himself said:

'We'll know our disinformation program is complete when everything the American public believe is false.'

And Malcolm X, human rights activist during the civil rights movement in America in the mid twentieth century, warned:

'If you're not careful, the newspapers will have you hating the people who are being oppressed and loving the people who are doing the

oppressing.'

And again, I have dealt with all of this in a previous book , - **'Puppets on a String',** - where I have gone into great detail about evidence given by various whistleblowers, such as Kevin Shipp, a CIA whistleblower, who confirmed that yes, governments are influencing viewing and reading content. He maintains that *'Mockingbird'* is still real. And yes, it started out as actually paying journalists in major meetings to print fake stories and interviews, - people being paid by CIA who are contributing to American journals.

It is still top secret how Mockingbird works today, or what it is now called. One notable sign that it still is in operation is the fact that U.S. media outlets and news organisations don't seem to compete with each other, they all report the same news in the same way! And the government gets no criticism from them! But one thing is for certain! It has presidents, senators, congressmen, judges, all in its pay-roll. Again, all obvious from the reports put out into the public arena by the media about who killed Kennedy and how evidence was manipulated, altered and covered up according to CIA dictates. And that still continues today!

But now at this present time, more and more people are awakening to the reality of what has been going on. Mainstream media are losing readers, listeners and viewers by the day. Parallel to this development we see all the more alternative media outlets get a larger foothold in the market; new news organisations and radio shows make for an alternative to understand what is going on inside the USA and throughout the world, for example Brian at London Real. Today we live in the golden age of trans-world communication where documents and photographs can be examined around the world in seconds, before they can be removed from public consumption!

Continuing declassification and information from whistleblowers is constantly alerting us to the fact that Mockingbird still exists. We live under the all-seeing eye of Big Brother, where everything we do to communicate with one another is closely monitored. We live in a world of high-tech, but unfortunately this all comes at a high price! Smart phones make dumb people! And dumb people can so easily be manipulated!

Mockingbird was started in the 1950s. Harper Lee published his novel *'To Kill A Mockingbird'* in 1960. What message was he giving us? Despite this, it is still a fact that today, the majority of people in the United States and throughout the world do not even know of the existence of Mockingbird!

And do not for one minute think that it is just in America! What happens in America spreads to the rest of the world very quickly! So of course we have Mockingbird in the BBC! The influence that the BBC exerts over us is unquantifiable. It boasted that by 2022, its services would have reached an estimated 500 million people worldwide. And the reach of its influence is extensive.

Everything, absolutely everything we read in the newspapers, we hear on the radio or watch on the television is the outcome of some strict form of processing, constantly exposing us to stress and making us more vulnerable. Ripe for controlling! And then the vultures move in!

'Above all else the BBC is an integral part of the British establishment. From its shockingly biased coverage of the General Strike back in 1926 through Suez and including the 2016 European Union Referendum, the BBC has been a dependable ally of the British government upon whom it

relies for the continuation of its royal charter ......money makes the BBC world go round. It pays for exorbitant salaries. It pays for eye-popping expense claims. It pays also for mouth-watering pension entitlements.' (David Sedgwick, *'BBC: Brainwashing Britain'* page 75)

And yes, money, money, money! That's why the likes of the UK's most prolific child abuser Jimmy Savile was harboured and protected by the BBC! Because he made them money! Treated as a celebrity, a do-gooder, given programmes to conceal his true identity, like *'Jim'll fix it',* treated as a national icon, a national treasure! It was an open secret at BBC what Saville was doing! Along with many others! And yet they promoted him and harboured him! Savile was an intimate of many of the western elite, including Britain's royal family, and even received an award from Pope John Paul II.

'Operation Yewtree' is a police investigation into sexual abuse allegations, predominantly the abuse of children, against the British media personality Jimmy Savile and others. The investigation, led by the Metropolitan Police Service, started in October 2012. After a period of assessment it became a full criminal investigation, involving inquiries into living people, notably other celebrities, as well as Savile.

The report of the investigations into the activities of Savile himself was published, as *'Giving Victims a Voice'*, in January 2013. Operation Yewtree continued as an investigation into others, some but not all linked with Savile. By October 2015, 19 people had been arrested by Operation Yewtree; seven of these arrests led to convictions. The *'Yewtree effect'* has been credited for an increase in the number of reported sex crimes, while the operation also sparked a debate on police procedure and rights of those accused of sex crimes. There is also *'Operation Hydrant', 'Operation Ravine'* and *'Operation Midland'.*

Mark Devlin, in his book, '*Musical Truth*', wrote:

'*The Savile exposure revealed how he had been sexually abusing children unimpeded for years, with some of the offences having taken place in his BBC dressing room. The suggestion that this could have gone on for so long without the knowledge of senior BBC management is inconceivable, particularly with 'celebrities' such as Esther Rantzen, Terry Wogan, Bill Oddie, Noel Edmonds and Paul Gabbaccini having acknowledged recently that Savile being a 'kiddie fiddler' was an 'open secret' within the Corporation. For Savile's 80th birthday, Prince Charles sent him a pair of gold cufflinks engraved with the words: 'No-one will ever know what you have done for this country, Jimmy!' At Savile's funeral, prior to his crimes being made public, former boxer Frank Bruno, (who Savile had introduced to his friend Peter Sutcliffe, aka The Yorkshire Ripper,) remarked that Savile had done 'a lot of good, special things that people don't even know' and that Savile 'helped me in a lot of ways that I can't really talk about on the television.' In June 2000, comedian Frank Skinner made what seemed to be a knowing reference to Savile's penchant for necrophilia in a live show. In a 1978 interview, Sex Pistols frontman Johnny Rotten remarked that he'd like to kill Jimmy Savile, saying: 'I bet he's into all kinds of seediness that we all know about but we're not allowed to talk about', adding, 'I know some rumours!' The general public, it seems, were the last to know.'* (Mark Devlin. '*Musical Truth*' page 38-39)

And Devlin further reports:

'.......*Savile was discovered to have abused children at the hospitals at which he 'volunteered', including disabled children in the spinal injuries unit of Stoke Mandeville hospital and inmates at Broadmoor Psychiatric Hospital. He was also exposed as a necrophiliac, having had sex with dead bodies in the mortuary of Leeds General Infirmary where he 'volunteered' as a night porter, (a claim made by fellow Radio 1 DJ Paul Gambaccini......before he himself was arrested on suspicion of historical sexual offences, but later released without charge.) Apparently no-one in BBC senior management had the slightest clue. Neither did the Queen when she awarded him an OBE in 1972 and as a Knight Bachelor in 1990. I'm sure it was all just one big misunderstanding. Savile's funeral was held on 9th November (or 9/11), but I'm sure that's just a coincidence.*

Savile is said to have been obsessed with Satanic practices, and some researchers have suggested he was a black magician, and hailed from a long-running bloodline of occulists.' (Mark Devlin, *'Musical Truth'* page 39)

And why else was Savile protected? Because he was a procurer of children! And closely associated with British royalty and Prime Ministers Edward Heath and Margaret Thatcher, whose government between 1979 and 1990 has been the focus of allegations about the Westminster paedophile ring.

In David Sedgwick's book *'The Fake News Factory'* already referred to, Sedgwick asks: *'What is happening to the BBC?'* And he points out:

'As of 2020, fewer people than ever trust the 'British' Broadcasting Corporation to tell the truth. Accusations of bias and fake news reverberate inside and outside of social media tarnishing the name of this once respected brand. Every minute of every day the BBC production line is hard at work. A finely-tuned machine, Britain's publicly-funded state broadcaster pumps out an enormous amount of content much of which attempts to mislead, unnerve and inflame the audience.

Encompassing its coverage of Trump, Brexit, climate change, Syria and everything in between, there is nothing spontaneous about propaganda. It is constructed to achieve specific goals.

Unable to modify its playbook by a single degree however, the corporation faces an existential crisis. More hated than loved, the BBC unravels in front of our eyes.'

And in Zena Cohen's book, *'The Shocking History of the EU'* we read:

'The BBC is not a broadcaster, it is a narrowcaster; a propaganda unit for the elite........

*The simple truth is that today's BBC is **Bi**ased, **B**ought and **C**orrupt and it isn't difficult to find the evidence showing this.'* (Zena Cohen,' *The Shocking History of the EDU'* page 80)

Cohen spells out this evidence:

'Before the Referendum was held, when the British people surprised and startled the Establishment by voting convincingly to leave the EU, the establishment media remained largely supportive of the EU and overtly, and sometimes cruelly, critical of those who had voted to leave the EU.

It isn't difficult to explain the media's enthusiasm for the European Union - though different branches of the media seem to have their own reasons for supporting an organisation which was founded by Nazis and which regards democracy as an unnecessary luxury.

The BBC has for years been consistently pro-EU and before the Referendum it was clear that the Corporation regarded the very idea of leaving the EU as sacrilegious. Even though the Corporation is funded by a compulsory licence fee taken from a largely unwilling and often rather resentful electorate, the BBC has deliberately favoured the minority point of view - the one expressed by Remainers.

In no area of politics has the BBC been so utterly devoted to one point of view as it has in the area of European integration.

In the months after the nation decided it no longer wanted to be ruled by a bunch of unelected bureaucrats living and working in Belgium, the BBC did everything it could to demonise Brexit and Brexiteers. On the relatively rare occasions when Brexit supporters were allowed into a studio, they were invariably labelled 'right wing' and treated as though they were in some way criminal. On the other hand, when Remainers were interviewed they were treated with great respect and introduced as though they were independent commentators.

It became quite well known that when the BBC arranged a programme with an audience then the audience would be packed with Remainers.

Every piece of bad news was (sometimes laughingly) blamed on Brexit and every piece of good news was accompanied by the phrase 'despite Brexit'. (Zina Cohen, 'The Shocking History of the EU' page 76-77)

The BBC has indeed shown that it is not impartial. As Cohen points out, between 2005 and 2015, the Today programme welcomed 4,275 guests to discuss the EU, of whom just 132 were Brexiteers.

'This has been going on for years. Way back in 2004, a study conducted by the Centre for Public Studies revealed that the BBC gave twice as much coverage to pro-EU speakers as to eurosceptics.

Since it has been established that the EU was created by Nazis to further the interests of Germany, it seems clear that the BBC has for years been supporting Nazi policies.' (Zina Cohen, 'The Shocking History of the EU' page 77)

And how else has the BBC shown itself to be blatantly pro-EU?

'The BBC even allows its anti-Brexit feeling to intrude on programmes which have nothing to do with news or politics. The 2018 edition of the Last Night of the Proms was ruined for many by the fact that television screens seemed to show interminable waving of EU flags. The 2019 BAFTA awards were edited and not shown as live but the BBC still managed to leave in anti-Brexit comments which for many viewers seemed jarring and utterly inappropriate.' (Zina Cohen, 'The Shocking History of the EU' page 79)

And as Zina Cohen concludes, along with countless others:

'It is, I think, now widely recognised that BBC journalists (like many of their colleagues working for other branches of the media) seem to have lost the ability to differentiate between 'news' and 'comment'.

Civitas, an independent think tank, has commented that 'the BBC pays lip service to impartiality but acts more like a political party with a policy manifesto.'

And there is no doubt, BBC is following CNN. CNN, 'The most trusted name in news', as their slogan goes! Sedgwick writes:

'Like its ideological British cousin, in matters political this omnipresent television network claims to be impartial. The links between the two organisations are indeed well established with the BBC regularly quoting from and using the network as a source for a proportion of its American output and vice versa. CNN's hysterical coverage of the Trump *presidency lurching to ever darker places, the bonds between the two channels become ever stronger.'* (David Sedgwick *'BBC: Brainwashing Britain'* page 85)

And a further example of fake news. Fake news being used this time to get public opinion behind the government in a war situation. A full-on, pro-war propaganda machine! David Sedgwick gives us an example of one British soldier's experience of how the BBC ensures the public receives only that message which it wishes them to receive:

'While serving in Iraq the BBC visited our camp to speak to troops. In a very strategic and careful move they made sure the soldiers they were going to speak to were going to tow the party line. Only hand-picked soldiers who were going to say the right things such as 'the Iraqis seem delighted we are here, we are making such a positive difference', were interviewed. All with the regiment's Commanding Officer stood in close proximity. Pretty intimidating for anyone who would dare to speak out having already agreed what they were going to say. Of course at the time of recording it was designed to look spontaneous in which of the troops they were speaking to and what they were saying, nothing could have been further from the truth.' (David Sedgwick, *'The Fake News Factory'* page 145)

And what about bias by omission? Very obvious in the reporting of the recent *'Black Lives Matter'* campaign and the death of George Floyd. BBC has termed him a *'gentle giant'*, but has completely disregarded his criminal record or the criminal record of the *'cop'* who supposedly killed Floyd. Nor that the funds of *'Black Lives Matter'* go to fund the American Democratic election campaign! A clear case of selective evidence to support a particular agenda. And this from a BBC that claims impartiality! Even the words used! *'rioters'* and *'protesters'* suggest two very different things. See how the broadcaster can so easily and craftily influence how several million people interpret or perceive any situation?

And bias by omission was very obvious as I watched a documentary on R.T.E on Tuesday 16th June 2020 at 11 p.m. and Tuesday 23rd June 2020, titled *'American Dynasties - The Bush Years.'* The programme depicted both father George Bush and boy George Bush as fuelled by ambition and driven by power, devoted to serving their country. Father George was shown as heroic for bailing out of his burning fighter plane over the Pacific Ocean on 2nd September 1944 and rescued by a US submarine. Yale university was mentioned, but not the *'Skull and Bones Society'* associated with Yale, and of which both father and son Bush were members. Nothing either of the *'Bohemian Club',* again, both of them being members. Or is this all just conspiracy theories? Conspiracy theory being, as we have seen, the dismissive term first used just after the assassination of President Kennedy in 1963, a term coined by the CIA itself to deflect any suggestion or thinking that the CIA were involved, and to throw people off from what they were actually doing. Any alternative to the *'lone gunman' theory* put forward by the Warren Commission was branded and dismissed as a *'conspiracy theory'*. A conspiracy theory since proved to be true!

And George Bush appointed as Director of CIA in 1975. He was portrayed in the same programme as building up the morale and the reputation of CIA, America's Intelligence Agency gone mad and under assault during the 1970s for the assassinations, coups, and the dirty tricks they were involved in. And here, in that documentary, was boy George Bush cleaning it all up! A massive propaganda exercise! And again, a prominent example of how the broadcaster can so influence how several million people interpret or perceive any situation or person.

The use of language to brain-wash and manipulate! Language like *'Almost certainly'*, *'most likely'*, *'it is probably correct to assume'*, *'it would appear that'* etc. all are used constantly to create a specific impression, to steer the reader along a pre-determined path in judgement.

And how to deflect criticism from yourself?

'Writing for 'Intercept', Glenn Greenwood recognises hypocrisy when he sees it. 'The most important fact to realise about this new term, those who most loudly denounce Fake News are typically those most aggressively disseminating it.' (David Sedgwick, *'BBC: Brainwashing Britain'* page 133)

The clever ploy of accusing the opposite side of that of which you yourself are guilty!

So *'fake news'*, *'lies'*, *'misrepresenting'*. What's the difference? - None whatsoever!

Take for example what happened on 9/11.

'The evidence to support the fact that 9/11 was, to a very large extent, an 'inside job' and not the work of 19 Arab hijackers arrived with box cutters directed by a man living in a remote cave on a dialysis machine, as the governments and mainstream media outlets of the world would have us believe, is monumental. The fact that at least five of the 'hijackers' are still alive is one. The idea that the incriminating paper passport of one of the 'hijackers' just happened to survive the carnage in

New York City intact, when all around steel and concrete had been pulverised to rubble is another. World Trade Center Building 7 standing intact behind BBC TV reporter Jane Standley as she announced it had collapsed a full 26 minutes before it actually did, and the BBC just happening to 'lose' their archive tapes of the broadcast is another. (You don't see much of Jane Standley on TV any more, do you? Funny that.) But you can take your pick from the several hundred other anomalies and discrepancies if you choose, as there's no shortage to select from, with the number of books, articles and videos now into the hundreds of thousands.

And all this from just one event. 9/11 is far from an isolated incident in terms of the big picture of what's really going on in our world, and the same anomalies with the 'official version' can be applied to pretty much every other major news event of the past several decades and beyond. While 'conspiracy theory' is a convenient catch-all term to dismiss any truthseeker who offers an alternative view to the official line, the majority of popular conspiracy 'theories' can now be demonstrated, with supporting evidence, to be conspiracy fact. And, in the twisted, inverted reality in which we find ourselves, it's the official government story which is the real 'conspiracy theory', laden as they are with glaring inaccuracies and discrepancies that make no sense under the scrutiny of a truly inquisitive and unbiased mind.' (Mark Devlin, *'Musical Truth'* page 9)

Fake news! It's everywhere! And fake news is the greatest threat to humanity!

We need to WAKE UP! To WAKE UP to the fact that our rights are slowly, gradually, but surely being taken away from us! And recently, in the midst of the world health crisis, this process was indeed intensified, with Facebook posts being removed, and our media being used to force us into obedience during the current lock-down, or should I say house-arrest! The free market place of ideas and free expression was closed down right in front of us. And it was closed down selectively. We complain about China and their lack of free press! But we are moving in the same direction, rapidly! Censorship here is extremely pervasive right now. People believe what they see on Netflix, for example, and don't understand that what they are watching is a censored version of the truth.

Note how the news programmes on mainstream channels during the lockdown, even the weather forecasts were all ending with *'Stay at home, stay safe, obey the rules!'* All manipulating us through fear! Fear that we had to obey the rules in order to be safe. The truth was that it became more obvious, by the day, that we were caught up in one of the greatest disinformation programmes ever inflicted on humanity!

All propaganda! Just like the propaganda in the gospels! Already mentioned! The gospels were written by the Romans as Roman propaganda against the Jewish peoples in the Roman-occupied Jewish territories! They had Jesus saying, *'Pay your taxes to Caesar!' 'Love your enemies!' 'Do good to those who persecute you!'* And Saint Paul telling slaves, *'Obey your masters!'* All propaganda with the aim of controlling!

But knowledge is power! And only by keeping us in ignorance can *'they'* continue to hoodwink us! It's all propaganda! And the chief medium of propaganda is the media!

Truth it seems, has gone out of fashion. The dishonesty of mass mainstream media knows no bounds. Indeed, we have been lied to now so much that the truth has become a victim of the State! The trouble is that when you tell the first lie, you have to keep telling lies in order to cover up that first lie. And so the lies continue, until you hang yourself with your own rope! And this is exactly what is happening all around us now! - Good news!

And more good news? As Mahatma Gandhi said:

'When I despair I remember that all through history the ways of truth and love have always won. There have been tyrants and murderers and for a time they can seem invincible, but in the end, they always fail. Think of it - always.'

Chapter 4:

So many secrets, so many cover-ups, so much subterfuge!

We cannot, and we must never, ever, underestimate the capability and capacity of our governments and all other institutions across the world to keep secrets and cover-ups!

How many times over just the last two years have we heard how politics is such a *'brutal game'*? Of course not all politicians can be tarred with the same brush, but there is no doubt that the world of politics is a dirty, murky world, and for one to survive one has to play the dirty, murky game!

A dirty murky game of so many secrets! So much subterfuge!

President J.F. Kennedy, speaking in April 1961 said:

'The very word 'secrecy' is repugnant in a free and open society; and we are as a people inherently and historically opposed to secret societies, to secret oaths and secret proceedings. We decided long ago that the dangers of excessive and unwarranted concealment of pertinent facts far outweigh the danger which are cited to justify it.'

And no doubt one of the greatest and best-kept secrets was the **Manhattan Project**.

The Manhattan Project is the perfect example of a black operation, a secret undercover project. For ten years, over two hundred thousand people worked on the development of the first atomic bomb, in eighty offices and dozens of production plants spread out across America, including a sixty-thousand-acre facility in rural Tennessee. And no one in Congress knew they existed until the atom bomb was dropped on Japan! It was eight days after the death of Franklin Roosevelt before Harry Truman knew these workers existed. And those putting each little bit together had no idea what the end product would look like, or for what purpose it was intended! Only those at the top knew that! And not at the top in the White House which is supposed to be the nerve-centre of everything. At the top of the military-industrial complex! The real power, the shadow government, the real power behind black operations!

Building the bomb was the single most expensive engineering project in the history of the United States. It began in 1942, and by the time the bomb was tested, inside the White Sands Proving Ground in the New Mexico high desert on 16th July, 1945, the bomb's price tag was over $28, 000,000,000. Not to mention the cost in lives that were to be lost!

And all surrounded by the thickest cloud of secrecy! Even Vice-President Harry Truman did not learn about the bomb's existence until he became president on 12th April 1945. As vice president, Truman had been the chairman of the Senate Special Committee to investigate the National Defense Program, which meant he was in charge of watching how money was spent during the war years, and yet he had no idea about the atomic bomb or its existence until he actually became president!

And who enlightened him? Vannevar Bush, his science advisor, and Harry L. Stimson, the nation's secretary of war. Bush was in charge of the Manhattan Project and Stimson was in charge of the war. That's how well they could all keep a secret!

While testing out and trying to harness the power of the atomic bomb, US scientists also secretly tested the bomb's effects on humans. During the Manhattan Project, which as we have just seen, gave way to the atomic bomb that destroyed Hiroshima and Nagasaki, US scientists resorted to secret human testing via plutonium injection on 18 unsuspecting, non-consenting patients. This included injecting soldiers with micrograms of plutonium for Project Oak Ridge along with later injecting three patients at a Chicago hospital. Out of the 18 patients, who were known only by their code-names and numbers at the time, only 5 lived longer than 20 years after injection.

Along with plutonium, researchers also experimented with uranium. At a Massachusetts hospital, between 1946 and 1947, Doctor William Sweet injected 11 patients with uranium. And who funded the same Doctor Sweet? The Manhattan Project! And in exchange for the uranium he received from the government, he would keep dead tissue from the body of the people he killed for scientific analysis on the effects of uranium exposure.

And '**Operation Paperclip'**, another covert, secret under-cover project! Operation Paperclip must surely rank as one of the dirtiest under-cover projects in American history!

This was a secret programme of the Joint Intelligence Objectives Agency (JIOA), largely carried out by Special Agents of Army CIC, primarily between 1945 and 1959, a secret programme involving the transference to the United States, of scientific expertise and technologies, including rocketry, pioneered and developed by Nazi scientists and engineers. Over 1,600 top-ranking Nazi space scientists, technicians, weapons and rocket engineers, including former leaders of the Nazi Party, and many who had been involved in medical experiments on Jewish prisoners in the Nazi concentration camps, together with their families, were brought to America, given American citizenship, and employed in the US space programme, in order for America to win the '*Race to the Moon*'. Hence it could be claimed that US scientists put the first man on the Moon.

So the primary purpose for Operation Paperclip was US military advantage over Russia in the Cold War and the Space Race. President Truman was persuaded by Eisenhower, the-then Supreme Allied Commander for Europe during and immediately after World War Two, and his military commanders, that America needed the advanced Nazi expertise in science and technology. Major-General Hugh deputy commander of the US Air Force in Europe stated:

'Occupation of German scientific and industrial establishments has revealed the fact that we have been alarmingly backward in many fields of research. If we do not take the opportunity to seize the apparatus and the brains that developed it and put the combination back to work promptly, we will remain several years behind while we attempt to cover a field already exploited.' (Taken from Michael Salla, '*Kennedy's Last Stand: Eisenhower, UFOs, MJ-12 and JFK's Assassination*' page 15)

The Joint Chiefs of Staff in late summer 1945 established the JIOA, a subcommittee of the Joint Intelligence Community, to directly oversee Operation Paperclip, formerly known as Operation Overcast. The top brass JIOA representatives included the army's Director of Intelligence, the Chief of Naval Intelligence, Assistant Chief of Air Staff-2 - Air Force Intelligence, and a representative from the State Department. In November 1945, Operation Overcast was renamed Operation Paperclip by Ordnance Corps, United States Army officers, who would attach a paperclip to the folders of those rocket experts whom they wished to employ in America.

Operation Paperclip! - Officially approved by President Truman in a **secret directive** circulated on September 3rd 1946, and expanded to include one thousand German scientists under *'temporary, limited military custody'*. But *'temporary, limited military custody'* was obviously a euphemism, a cover, for gainful employment in the American science and space industries.

And so while the rest of the world watched in shock, horror and disbelief, as Nazi crimes were exposed, and while the Nuremberg trials were investigating the abuse of ethics and rights of humanity, the United States of America was secretly taking in Nazi scientists and giving them American identities! And the world knew nothing about it!

Nazi scientists and engineers, including those who had worked in the infamous human experiments, - experiments which included butchering of children, especially twins and dwarfs, - performing unspeakable experimental procedures, such as removing nerves from people's bodies without anaesthetic, conjoining twins, changing eye colour and shape, changing skin pigmentation, re-arranging hands and feet, and testing explosion effects on humans in Germany, were now brought to America with *'their talents'* to work in a number of top secret projects for the United States!

Those who should have been facing justice by trial and the most severe punishment for their inconceivable crimes! - These same now given faked political biographies, their past crimes obliterated from all records as if they had never happened! These same now allowed to live as free men, continuing to indulge their various passions in a life-style which would have been the envy of many! Men like Wernher von Braun, along with his V-2 rocket team! Werner von Braun now to become NASA engineering programme manager and chief architect of the Apollo Saturn V.

And all kept tightly under wraps! Not for human consumption!

And indeed, not just America, but Russia too! The Soviet Union recruited more than 2,200 German specialists—a total of more than 6,000 people including family members—with Operation Osoaviakhim during one night on October 22, 1946.

The spoils of war! There for the picking! And the taking!

And the obvious reason why President Kennedy could so confidently assert on 12th September 1962, that America would have a man on the Moon by the end of the decade was because he knew he had the full weight of Nazi technology, science and rocketry know-how in his camp!

And what happened to Hitler? We have always been led to believe that he was found dead in that bunker along with Eva Braun. Really?

In 1952, Dwight D. Eisenhower wrote:

'We have been unable to unearth one bit of tangible evidence of Hitler's death. Many people believe that Hitler escaped from Berlin.'

When President Truman asked Joseph Stalin at the Potsdam Conference in 1945 whether or not Hitler was dead, Stalin replied bluntly, *'No'*. Stalin's top army officer, Marshall Gregory Zhukov, whose troops were the ones to occupy Berlin, flatly stated after a long and thorough investigation in 1945:

'We have found no corpse that could be Hitler's.'

The chief of the US trial council at Nuremberg, Thomas J. Dodd, said:

'No one can say he is dead.'

Lieutenant General Bedell Smith, Chief of Staff to General Eisenhower in the European Invasion and later Director of the CIA, stated publicly on October 12th, 1945,

'No human being can say conclusively that Hitler is dead.'

And Colonel W.J Heimlich, former Chief, Unites States Intelligence, at Berlin, stated for publication that he was in charge of determining what had happened to Hitler and after a thorough investigation his report was:

'There was no evidence beyond that of HEARSAY to suport the THEORY OF HITLER'S DEATH.'

So what happened to Hitler? And why have we not been told? Why the huge **secret**?

Many historians now claim that Hitler spent the remainder of his life in Argentina, supported and kept safe by those with whom he had built up close alliances. And the two bodies in the bunker? If not those of Hitler and Eva Braun, then who? -   DECOYS!

And all kept quiet and under wraps because the Allies could not admit that they let Hitler get away, - and under their very noses! They had to save face! And saving face is what some of the keeping of secrets by governments appears to be about! As we will see again with Matt Hancock in the next chapter!

OR! Was some sort of secret deal done with Hitler that allowed him to get away?

And what happened to the Nikola Tesla papers? Nikola Tesla who believed he had found the key to free energy! Free energy? Free electricity? Just think how many less millionaires there would be in the world today if we all had free electricity! Just think how many individuals and corporations would be losing out on fortunes! So it is not rocket science to work out why Tesla's papers were mysteriously removed from the hotel room in New York where he was living, - the Hotel New Yorker, - and have never been seen since! *'Men In Black'* arrived before Tesla's nephew could get there! And *'Men In Black'* spells government! Secrecy! Subterfuge!

So many secrets! So much subterfuge! - Antarctica! Underwater bases! Flying saucer programmes! The truth about Roswell! Operation Majestic - MJ12; Kennedy's assassination! Project Sign 1947; Project Grudge 1949; Project Blue Book 1952; The secret Greada Treaty between Eisenhower and an extraterrestrial race; the part played by the Vatican in the negotiations with extraterrestrials! Area 51! 9:11! The war in Iraq! The war in Syria! Brexit! What happened on the moon? What were those bases found there? And the recent pandemic! What cover-ups are about to be uncovered about all of this? And the truth about the lock-down? Who was responsible for what? The secrets behind Bohemian Grove, - where US presidents are selected! Free Masons! The symbolism of the Eagle! The truth about the symbol of the serpent! The secrets hidden in the American $1 bill! The secrets hidden in the architecture of our great cities!

And all of this is only scratching the surface! It goes on and on, - and on! And all explained in my previous book *'**Out Of The Darkness Of Deception And Despair - Into The Light Of Truth'**,* published in 2021.

And of course, all those mysterious and unexplained deaths! For example, the mysterious death of John Forrestal, May 1949. The first instance of a senior political figure being killed to maintain the UFO coverup! The same Forrestal, who knew so much about the UFO coverup and was giving information to Kennedy! Forrestal, sacked by Truman and died shortly afterwards in mysterious circumstances! Marilyn Monroe! - Suicide or murder? And I have gone into detail about all of this in previous books:

- **'Homo SPACIENS: We Are Not From Planet Earth! - Our Connection with UFOs, ETs and Ancient Civilisations'**

- **'Those Strange Looking Men in Their Flying Machines: Visitors From Beyond Time and Space? Or From Planet Earth? ETs, UFOs, and Who Knows What'**

- **'Above Our Heads: Predators or Protectors?'**

Even the cover-up about William Shakespeare! Yes! THEE WILLIAM SHAKESPEARE! The one-and-only! The same one-and-only who never actually existed! And again, I have covered all of this in 2 of my previous books, **'To Be Or Not To Be..........The Man of Stratford who was never to be Shakespeare: Exposing the deception that was William Shakespeare'** and **'If Not Shakespeare, Then Who? Unmasking the Real Bard of Avon!'**

So Shakespeare NOT Shakespeare? To topple a stalwart, an icon like Shakespeare, from his literary pedestal, is that not surely tantamount to sacrilege, blasphemy, profanity? To expose Shakespeare as not being Shakespeare, but a deception and a fraud, is surely enough to cause not just shock waves, but an entire tsunami! *'Oh Horror! Horror! Horror!'*

But the person who wrote the Shakespeare works was writing under a pseudonym! A case of identity theft! So, why have we not been told? Why has the deception been continued?

The myth of Shakespeare, and that is all it is, has been built entirely around the lucrative tourist trade in Stratford-upon-Avon. Just like the tourist spots in Israel, associated with the story of Jesus in the gospels! All big money tourist traps! All big, big, big business! All big, big, big money spinners!

And here in our own country, - St. Patrick! The story of St. Patrick driving the serpents out of Ireland! St. Patrick's Day, 17th March, - THEE big money spinning day in Ireland. THEE big tourist attraction! The day when the whole world goes green! Even the sheep in the fields!

But the truth? The truth that has been hidden under wraps for centuries! Patrick, the Roman, the son of a Roman official, - tasked with bringing Christianity to Ireland! Christianity that drove out the Druids, our native ancient ancestors. All part of the plan to promote Christianity as the dominant religion of the world. All part of the cleansing! The cleansing that led to countless deaths and the destruction of so many valuable ancient tests! The *'snakes'* , - symbolic of the *'pagans,'* the Druids! St Patrick's Day! - Symbolic of the victory of Christianity over the Old Religion and beliefs, stemming from the ancient Gnostic and Egyptian teachings and beliefs.

But! - Where did Patrick find the snakes? Our climate here is most certainly not conducive to snakes! And never was! So *'snakes'* was the metaphor for the pagans and Druids. Just as the early Gnostics were referred to as *'snakes' and* demonised by that same new Christian Church.

And the symbolism of the serpent or snake? - Initially the serpent was a symbol of the ultimate balance of knowledge, energy and spirituality. And new life! - The serpent sheds its skin. But corrupted by Christianity to represent and symbolise the very opposite! As shown in the biblical story of the serpent in the Garden of Eden!

St. Patrick's Day! A wild extravaganza! A great day of fun! But underneath the false surface, the veneer, the facade, lurks the darkness! Leprechauns, parades, festivities, alcohol, promotion of all things Irish! But the truth lies hidden beneath! Just like the glitter and sparkle of the circus ring! Beneath all the glamour and exciting up-beat *'roll-up'* music, there often lurks a life of pain and misery for the animals! But it all makes money! - *'It's the economy, stupid!'*

And of course, at this point in time, the greatest government cover-up concerns UFOs and extraterrestrial life forms!

Nick Pope is a freelance British journalist and media commentator. He was an employee at the British Government's Ministry of Defence from 1985 to 2006 and is best known for a role he undertook for the British Government from 1991 to 1994, which involved investigating reports of UFO sightings to determine their defence significance. He moved to the United States in January 2012. At the time, while the Ministry of Defence stated that it *'remains totally open-minded about the existence or otherwise of extraterrestrial lifeforms'*, it also stated that there was no evidence to suggest that any UFO sightings posed any threat to the UK or that they were extraterrestrial in origin. It is clear from the material that Pope wrote whilst still at the MOD that he did not share the MOD's view that conventional explanations could be found for all UFO sightings. Pope's final posting in the MOD was to the Directorate of Defence Security. He resigned in 2006, saying that the government's

'*X files have been closed down*', and in 2009, MOD announced that UFO sightings would no longer be investigated. Pope continues his research and investigation in a private capacity and now works as a freelance journalist and media commentator, covering subjects that include the unexplained, space, conspiracy theories, science fiction and fringe science. He has appeared in multiple TV History Channel's '*Ancient Aliens' and* multiple episodes of '*UFOs Declassified'.* Also on Canada's *History Television*. His books include '*Open Skies, Closed Minds', 'The Uninvited',* 'and '*Encounter in Rendlesham Forest*'. In his books, Pope openly discusses the politics surrounding the way in which those within government and the military view UFO phenomena.

Together with other well-known names in this same area, - amongst them being Mary Rodwell, David Jacobs, Clifford Stone, Dan Sherman, Lyn Buchanan, Melinda Leslie, - Nick Pope took part in a recent Sky History documentary on 12th March 2023. In that documentary it was made perfectly clear that governments are covering up about the existence of UFOs, extraterrestrial life and the fact that contact has been made and is on-going with extraterrestrials who have advanced technology.

Also made very clear was about how our DNA has been, and is being manipulated. And how the most ancient texts such as the Book of Enoch, and the Apocryphon of John for example, have been left out of the church gospels in just the same way as the Council of Nicea left out the Gospel of Philip, the Gospel of Thomas, the Gospel of Mary Magdalene and all the others found at Nag Hammadi. - Simply because they did not fit the narrative of this new Roman Christian Church founded by Emperor Constantine!

The point was strongly made that whoever controls space, controls the planet. The truth has now been diluted to such an extent that it is hardly recognisable anymore. Pope explained how governments are corporations, money-making institutions, all millionaires and billionaires, all Public School boys, and of course, all from secret boys' clubs. They are selected because they will keep the system going that sustains them. The system that keeps them in power and wealth and the system for keeping things quiet.

Pope furthermore brought up about the deep concern that various presidents, - Truman and Eisenhower in particular, - had about multiple projects and the massive competing departments within government. Departments all doing their own thing, following their own agenda, and definitely not united as a government. All private corporations, with massive control over governments in fact. And these private corporations are using governments as cover security.

Also on the same programme was Clifford Stone, retired from the US Army and now an author. Stone confirmed that the aliens visiting earth were referred to as *'our guests'*. And he also confirmed being called to an incident, where a UFO craft had crashed and lay in a ditch, with a dead entity lying on the ground along with several non-human bodies. The process of recovering all of this was classified as *'Project Moondust'*, and definitely Top Secret. In his book *'Eyes Only - The Story of Clifford Stone and UFO Crash Retrievals',* Stone tells of his experiences working as a UFO crash retrieval expert with the US Army. In a review of his book, Carol Rosin, founder of the Institute for Security and Cooperation in Outer Space writes:

'Sgt. Clifford Stone is one of the most important truth tellers of our time. This book is a collector's treasure of his unique personal experieces in the military with real extraterrestrial beings. I recognize his truth and

honor him for having the courage to tell it. Clifford carries a time-sensitive and world changing message vital to our very survival, that 'they are not hostile'. His story educates and opens doors to a new awareness about what's really going on behind veils of secrecy which influence all our lives.'

And with reference to evidence about ETs, Stone makes the point:

'The absence of evidence does not mean the evidence of absence'.

Dan Sherman spent almost three years as an *'intuitive communicator'* while serving in the USAF. In his book, *'Above Black'*, Sherman tells of his training, things he learned from his alien contacts and the events that led him to seek a discharge from the United States Air Force. On that same programme, Sherman confirmed yet again that the whole UFO and ET saga has nothing to do with political leaders but with the military. With them all is *'Above Top Secret'*. Top secret black projects. Then grey is even further above black, apparently.

By coming forward, Sherman has said that he hopes his story will encourage other insiders to do likewise. He says: *'The information I have come forward with is important in the sense that someone has to start talking.....someone from the inside. Preserve Destiny is only one of many alien projects that I suspect the US governments, as well as other governments, are heavily involved with. In releasing to the public what I know, I have tried to take a stand against the keepers of the grey flame within the sacred halls of the NSA, CIA, USAP, NRO and other agencies. Hopefully, this book will open the door for other insiders to peer through and feel more comfortable stepping forward into the light of day. If not, 'they' will continue to suppress the most fascinating aspects of our own existence....that others exist.'*

Sherman's story, which was first told to him when he joined the USAF, and not before, is that his mother was visited by aliens in the summer of 1960, in a random test programme between US military and aliens to determine compatibility between humans and aliens. In that genetic management programme with certain aliens, Sherman inherited, through his mother and what was done to her, an ability to communicate through the intuitive manipulation of the mind, obviously something on the lines of telepathy. And when he began to work, he was communicating with an alien called '*Bones*'. Apparently, according to Sherman, in 1947 the US government made contact with an alien species - known today as '*greys*'. The experiment was named '*Project Preserve Destiny*', a genetic management project with the sole purpose of cultivating human offspring so that they would have the ability to communicate with the greys. Sherman's mother was initially abducted in 1960 for tests, and then again in 1963 for the actual genetic procedure while Sherman was in her womb. That meant that Sherman had certain abilities as he was a product of Project Preserve Destiny. He left the USAF after twelve years because he could no longer carry the heavy burden of secrecy, loneliness and isolation that was so much a part of the work. For him, it was either leave, or go completely insane.

Lynn Buchanan, also on the same programme, worked as a remote viewing expert, - a military person doing data-based work. He confirmed that many government officials and senators would come to his department to ask about contact with ETs. But the answer was always the same - a resounding '*No!*' However, he also said that even though the answer to government officials or senators was a firm '*No!*', when it was a private company he was dealing with, the information was handed over.

One of the main questions asked on that programme was about how many military men carry the burden of secrecy? It must certainly be a heavy burden to keep the greatest secret in the world, - the secret that we are '*not alone*', - when one has sworn security oaths.

Another question asked was about how far do officials actually go to manipulate the masses? And in doing this, Pope explained how language is always so important. Just one word can make all the difference, or the juxtaposition of one word against another, - all effective in changing the meaning, with defensive words and phrases. For example, the use of the phrase '*flying saucer*' makes it all sound outdated, and therefore in the past, so no point in bothering with it! Words matter in the murky world of government and the language they speak. And sometimes what they do not say can be even more important.

So why now? Why are we getting all these insider views of what has been going on in government? Since 2014 there has been an increase in these occurrences, according to Nick Pope. 2014 in fact marked a turning point in government disclosures. Up until then the language of governments with regard to ET and UFO disclosures was the language of hostility and conflict. The French government opened their files in 2007, followed by the British government in 2008. But this mostly disclosed just letters from the public about sightings!

But now, the phenomenon is real. Everybody knows that! And inside governments, the view has shifted from ridiculing to taking an interest in abductees.

So the narrative has changed! The whole phenomenon cannot be ignored any longer! We are in the 21st Century, - not in 1950. And the public is pushing for the release of UFO information. So the governments are responding by trying to bring it all out in a way that makes it sound realistic and grounded. The secrets just cannot be kept any longer! We are in new territory now, and the government language has changed. Changed from **U**nidentified **F**lying **O**bjects to **U**nidentified **A**erial **P**henomenon. And their aim is now for controlled disclosure. The UFO phenomenon has been re-branded! And with this re-branding, they will control the narrative! They can pretend that old history never happened! And so there was no cover-up of any kind!

But the public know there was!

Another programme that was aired just recently was on Blaze TV channel, on Monday evening, 27th March 2023, a two hour special, called *'William Shatner meets Ancient Aliens'*. That's the very same William Shatner, famous for his role in *'Star Trek'*. He was joined in the programme by several of the leading experts of *'Ancient Aliens'*, - Nick Pope, David Childress, Giorgio Tsoukalos, Richard Dolan, and on video by Eric von Däniken.

Amongst other topics discussed was the origins of human existence and the ground-breaking archaeological finds that are giving us a new understanding of the cosmos and how we are not alone!

Then on the same channel on Friday 31st March, Area 51 was discussed, and Bob Lazer who blew the whistle on Area 51 confirmed about the alien technology with which he worked, and the government's war to silence him.

Also discussed was the whole area of astronaut encounters with extraterrestrials. And how, to this day, NASA still denies UFO accounts and has taken measures to prevent astronauts from telling their stories.

So it is obvious they are indeed hiding something! But what?

It was made very clear too that Government and Military have been turning a blind eye to reports of UFO sightings, as in Socorro New Mexico, and Louisville Kentucky, and so the story dies the next day. Civilian UFO witnesses as well as police officers have all been met with deafening silence, detectives turning their heads and looking the other way, all in an attempt to destroy these people's credibility and make them look like fools.

But! The proverbial genie is out of the bottle! And it is definitely NOT for going back in! The sluice gates have opened! All that was hidden is being revealed!

And as this book goes to press, on another Blaze TV Channel documentary programme, on Sunday 16th April 2023, with Craig Charles, it was made clear by Nick Pope again, that the evidence now is so overpowering that UFOs and extraterrestrials can no longer be kept secret. Directives have been given by the Pentagon to all military men who might encounter UFOs, - so does that not prove that they must indeed actually exist?

Furthermore, on the same programme, videos of UFOs captured on military systems were shown, some over the Atlantic, some over the Pacific, with images showing crafts with no identifying marks, no wings, and no obvious methods of propulsion, travelling at enormous speeds, disappearing into the water and then out again, before disappearing into space again. Performing manoevers that defy all known physics! Such examples were witnessed from the navy vessel 'USS Princeton' in 2004, 'USS Nimritz' and 'USS Theodore Roosevelt' in 2015, - all documented under government files such as 'Gofast', 'Gimbal',

'*Pyramid*' '*TicTac*', - and all now released into the public domain by the Pentagon. The question is, are these all enemy advanced technology, some human adversary leap-frogging in the technology field? Or are they from another world? No one knows! Or, as Nick Pope theorised, is there possibly a super-predator species out there somewhere, and are these craft looking for some sort of safe haven for self-preservation? Space refugees coming here? Again, no one knows!

Of the recent 144 investigations done by the Pentagon, only one craft was identified as '*man made*'. The other 143? - An '*ET explanation could not be ruled out*'!

There is now an increasing '*leaking*' campaign going on, with the Pentagon confirming their authenticity. So political pressure for full disclosure in the US is mounting! But, as Pope believes, the government is still holding most of it back, keeping it all within government, still hiding a lot, - in fact we are only getting about one in a thousand of what is out there! So we must ask, are governments colluding and negotiating with extraterrestrials?

But! We are now on a journey to find the truth! We need to know! No matter what that truth is, we have a right to know, we deserve to know! This is a new reality we are now living in, where we just do not know what is going on in the skies above us. Are these unidentified craft manned craft? Robots? Advanced probes?

No more secrets! No more subterfuge! No more cover-ups!

Happy days!

Chapter 5:

Irretrievable loss of trust

'There is nothing hidden that will not be revealed!' - The main theme of this book!

All the back-stabbing, all the insult-slinging, all the word-play, all the manipulation, all the lies, all the denials, all the deceit, - when we consider all that goes on in politics, in every political party, then is it any wonder that the vast majority of people have completely lost any sort of trust in their government? It has become increasingly clear that politics and politicians are all about self-preservation!

And what we have witnessed over the last recent traumatic years, during the so-*called 'pandemic',* has only served to distance and alienate people even further from politicians and the murky world of politics.

Matt Hancock, former Health Secretary at the height of the '*Covid-19 pandemic*', and other government ministers and officials have all been exposed in the recently leaked more than 100,000 messages sent between them. Referred to as the '*WhatsApp leaks',* they have been obtained by the Telegraph newspaper.

These disclosures, and Matt Hancock's performance in the recent '*I'm a Celebrity! Get me out of here!*' all give us an ugly insight into the workings and thinkings of government. They expose the egotism, the superficiality, the narcissism, the hypocrisy, the lies, the lust for power, the sheer pig-headedness, the manipulations, the distortions, the cover-ups, the arrogance, the vanity, the indiscretions, the one-rule-for-them-another-rule-for-us, the falsifications of the truth, the unwillingness to admit that possibly they might have got it wrong, the u-turns, the propaganda, the coercion, the threats, the false hope, the adrenalin of power, the pathetic attempts at justification, the scare-mongering tactics, the scare-mongering posters appearing on our streets, - Matt Hancock announcing '*If you go out, people will die*' and slogans constantly and everywhere thrust into our face such as '*Save the NHS*' , '*If you hug your granny, you'll kill her*' , '*Stay at home*', '*Hands, face, space*' - strikingly similar to the children's nursery rhyme '*Hands, knees and bumps-a -daisy!*'

'*Save the NHS*'! The NHS was on its knees long before '*Covid-19*' ever hit! And the government did that all on its own, with no input whatsoever from the public! And all those false declarations and accolades coming from the lips of government officials! And now, more than two years later, NHS staff have still not got a pay rise! All their dedication to duty, their profound and genuine love for the work they do, - all taken for granted. So you see, it's just words, words, words! All meaningless! Because that's what governments do! They play on the good will of the people for whom they should be working!

WAKE UP!

And then all the confusion in the conflicting orders - '*Stay at home.....go out to get food, to exercise.... go to work.....don't go to work* ', etc. etc. etc And then of course, '*Go out to eat out!*' What could the rationale behind this possibly have been? After ordering us to stay indoors and isolated from other people, now we get this! Nothing making any kind of sense!

Not to mention the coercion, the bribery and intimidation tactics, - offering free ice-cream, free pizzas or free concert tickets to young people if they got the jab! And the fines if caught outside of a certain radius, not adhering to social distancing, not wearing masks, going for a walk with a takeaway coffee in hand, etc. etc. etc.

The fear instilled into people! But as we have seen, instilling fear was at the root of all the government ploys and tactics. Hancock's self-expressed aim - '*We frighten the pants off everyone with the new strain.*'

Let me repeat that! - '**We frighten the pants off everyone!**' Hancock proudly declaring that he wanted news of the Alpha variant timed to create maximum fear, while Simon Case, the Cabinet Secretary, cheered from the side-lines, assuring Hancock, '*The fear/guilt factor vital*'. And Hancock's special adviser, '*It's not unhelpful having people think they could be next.*'

And of course the bully-boy oppressive tactics! In response to any criticism or resistance! Hancock threatening an MP who intended to vote against him that he would withdraw government financial support for a learning disability hub in that particular constituency!

The then Prime Minister, Boris Johnson, - derided as the '*wonky shopping trolley*' by Dominic Cummings, - thinking it '*superb*' that two travellers had been fined £10,000 for evading quarantine regulations. And Matt Hancock gloating over returning travellers who were forced to quarantine in basic hotels at their own expense as a result of yet another changing of rules, all of which Simon Case regarded as '*hilarious*'.

Who can forget the farcical performance of Matt Hancock in the jungle in *'I'm a Celebrity! Get me out of here!'*? How he disclosed that politicians are all taught how to '*Pivot*', - how to avoid a question by diverting it back to something positive about themselves. Yes, sure we all knew that! But the fact that they took us all for fools! That's the most insulting part! Them thinking we don't know their ploys and tactics!

Yes, Hancock managed to win and bring the stars back to camp. But look how! By being able to turn his feelings and emotions off when all sorts of insects and creepy crawlies were all over him! He was able to block all of this out! In just the same way as he was able to turn off all feelings and emotions when he was causing pain and untold misery to thousands upon thousands of people with his instructions about no visits to care homes, no visiting dying relatives and no attending funerals. And the pain and suffering of those countless cancer and other patients denied treatment! And the misery caused by the closure of small businesses! It all reminds me of the film '*Blade Runner*', a 1982 science fiction film adapted from Philip K. Dick's 1968 novel *'Do Androids Dream of Electric Sheep?'* The film is set in a dystopian future Los Angeles of 2019, in which synthetic humans known as replicants are bio-engineered by the powerful Tyrell Corporation to work on space colonies. When a fugitive group of advanced replicants led by Hauer escapes back to Earth, burnt-out cop Ford reluctantly agrees to hunt them down. And the memorable and poignant words come to mind: *'You have done alright until now! - Without having a soul!'*

Soul-less! Does that describe Matt Hancock? Or any other of our politicians?

The same Hancock who resisted shortening the 14-day quarantine period in spite of scientific advice that the 5 days was enough. And his reasoning? It would make them look weak! Admitting that he had inflicted untold damage on a whole society by mistake? And at all costs, having to save face!

And when it was suggested to him that once the vaccine rollout started the lockdown should be relaxed, - what was Hancock's reply? - *'This is not a SAGE call. It's a political call.'*

Hancock no doubt saw the pandemic as a chance for his political career: *'A well-handled crisis of this scale could propel you into the next league'* as a *'wise friend'* told him. And then his declaration in the jungle that he broke no laws when caught on camera in an intimate embrace with his lover behind the office door! He broke no rules, - because they were only *'Guidelines'!*

Guidelines? So they were never rules then? So why were we told that they were? And how could so many people have been fined for breaking *'guidelines'?*

And when Hancock left the jungle, one of the first questions he asked? *'Did I come across as authentic?'* And of course, *'I think I look great',* and *'thousands of people voted for me.'*

And in another newly-released leaked message, Boris Johnson spoke of the need to get *'absolutely militant'* on social distancing in Covid hotspots, saying there had been a *'general collapse'* in *'rule'* following. Furthermore, in a WhatsApp conversation with Simon Case from July 2020, he wrote: *'We need to tell people that if they want to save the economy and protect the NHS then they need to follow the rules.'*

Follow the rules? How ironic! When those who made them were breaking them right, left and center!

'And we may need to tighten the rules. You can now have six people from different households indoors. Do people really understand that and are they observing it?' Johnson asked.

This exchange came one month after the prime minister broke the rules himself. Johnson, his wife Carrie, and the then-chancellor, Rishi Sunak, all received a fine for attending a birthday party thrown in the ex-PM's honour in June 2020.

And now, just recently, Home Secretary Suella Braverman! At the heart of the Home Secretary's responsibility is to ensure that the laws are fully enforced for all. And what has she just done? Caught for speeding, she asked her civil servants if they could arrange a private one-to-one driving awareness course for her rather than attend the group course with other motorists. They refused and reported the request to the Cabinet Office. Braverman then asked one of her political aides to assist her, following which requests (which were refused) were made to the course providers requesting use of an alias, or for her camera to be switched off. So! Speeding fine and seeking special treatment! She has also been accused of authorising her special adviser to tell journalists that there was no speeding penalty, - when there was!

Why are we no longer surprised?

And of course we had *'Golfgate'* here in Ireland! In Clifden, Connemara where all the big brass were gathered for a golf dinner! No sign of any rules, - oops! - Guidelines there!

It goes on and on, - scandal after scandal after scandal. Partygate, of course, being one of the greatest! Prime Minister and Rishi Sunak both amongst those fined for breaking rules, and Sunak later fined further for not wearing a seat belt! And the corruption and scams in dishing out contracts to friends for supply of medical equipment and vaccines! Corruption, corruption, corruption!

So many instances that came to light where those very same people, who made the restrictive and suffocating rules for the rest of us, were, all that time, failing to adhere to those same rules themselves!

As Simon Case admitted, in one of his more indiscreet messages, by 2021 public distrust of Johnson was too strong for his words to carry any weight. And not just public distrust of Johnson, - but for all of the government! A failed government in every respect!

And the vaccination programme that was rolled out? What exactly was that all about? It is time we questioned it! It is time to demand accountability!

A vaccination, surely, is meant to provide immunity? Is that not what we have always been led to believe and expect? That if we get vaccinated, then we will not catch that particular virus, disease or whatever it is meant to be? Is a vaccination not supposed to be a preparation of a tiny amount of the actual virus or bacteria, or whatever, to provide the body's natural immune system with the opportunity to create antibodies to ward off a greater dose of that same particular virus? Hence, one could expect immunity. And certainly, it cannot be denied that previous vaccination programmes have been used effectively to fight deadly diseases.

But! This more recent vaccination programme rolled out to an unsuspecting public? How come a second, and a third, and a fourth, and now a fifth jab are deemed necessary? And all within a very short period of time? And how come all this even though the actual killer 'virus' that was supposed to be 'Covid-19' was never actually identified and isolated? And how come so much threatening, forcing, persuading, cajoling, stick and carrot were all necessary? Not to mention the punishments meted out? And the marginalisation and castigation of those who refused to get 'vaxxed? Surely, as sovereign beings, each and every one of us has the undisputed right to decide what we put into our own body? And the threats of having to have a 'Covid passport' in order to travel? And how come so many people, after getting all four vaccinations still came down with Covid? And how come so many died? What happened to immunity for all of these people?

And the falsification of numbers! All admitted later! Algorithms, projections, predictions, - it went on and on and on! Nothing making sense! And the recorded reactions and health conditions that are arising from the vaccination! All exposed in Pfizer's own recent shocking report!

And now what? How come it is now never mentioned? Where did it all go? And how come so many people are now dying, more so than during the actual 'pandemic'?

Surely it is not rocket science to work out what is staring us in the face, - that this recent vaccination can NOT have been a vaccination? So if it was not a vaccination, then what actually was it? Somebody somewhere has the answers, but we are not being told!

And just recently, Tue May 9, 2023, Wide Awake Media and LifeSiteNews, neither of them mainstream media, reported that former Vice President at Pfizer, Dr. Mike Yeadon, who spent 32 years working mostly for large pharmaceutical companies, spoke about the sequence of events which led him to conclude that the so-called '*pandemic*' was planned and co-ordinated in advance, by unelected globalist bodies like the WHO and WEF, as a justification to deliberately depopulate the planet via the lethal mRNA injections:

'*We're facing something much worse than an alleged virus. The injuries to people from these so called vaccines... I wish I could tell you that it was accidental, but it wasn't accidental. I'm convinced that these injections have been made to injure people, to maim and kill deliberately.... Multiple obvious toxicities were deliberately built into the alleged vaccines' designs, with the result that there would be high expectations of blood clots, autoimmune attacks and cytokine storms all over the body, depending on where it went in a given individual.*'

Reviewing how he came to understand the COVID '*pandemic*' was something other than what it appeared to be, the pharmacology expert recalled that '*when I started noticing former colleagues of mine, including Patrick Vallance, saying things on the television I knew weren't true — and I knew he knew weren't true — that's when the penny dropped for me, probably February 2020.........I remember saying to my wife, 'this is not what they're saying it is. Something's going on,.........And when I saw not only my country locking down, but dozens of countries locking down at the same time … that was proof, and is still proof, of a supranational operation,......There's no way that could have happened at the local level, at the country level. Therefore, it must have occurred at a level above. Whether it was the WHO or the World Economic Forum, or other, I don't know, but the orchestrated response demonstrates a planned event as opposed to one determined by the chance of the virus developing.........These governments all did the same stupid, ineffective, known-not-to-work things at the same time, none of which were in their countries' pandemic preparedness plans, because I've read them all.'*

Further, he said that he is perfectly confident he will not be sued by Vallance or others for publicly accusing them of lying, because they know they would lose in a court of law. *'And so, they won't sue me. What they do is smear me and censor me.'*

'Get the jab!' Thundered out to us from every poster, every television programme, even the *'soaps'*! Everywhere we went, - there it was!

And most people complied! Most people rolled up their sleeve! In blind obedience to the orders given!

And why? Simply because of fear. Sheer terror! And because they trusted their governments! The fear that was instilled into humanity! All part of the plan! All part of the agenda! As Bill Gates himself said:

'This is not a vaccine story. This is a population management story.'

The same Bill Gates who has openly declared vaccines to be:

'The best investment I've ever made.'

The same Bill Gates, the spear-head of the eugenics programme! The same Bill Gates described by a Geneva-based NGO representative:

'He is treated like a head of state, not only at the WHO, but also at the G20.'

The same Bill Gates, self-appointed expert on health, and with no medical qualifications whatsoever! The same Bill Gates who founded Microsoft! Who controls WHO! And I have dealt with all of this in *'**Out Of The Darkness of Deception and Despair - Into the Light of Truth'**,* published in 2021.

And remember the Thalidomide babies born back in the mid 20th century? The Thalidomide drug that was administered to pregnant women! As a treatment for morning sickness! And even though there had been no trials run with pregnant women!

Thalidomide was sold as an over-the-counter medication, under the name 'Contergan', and first promoted as an aide for people with anxiety and trouble sleeping. Well over 10,000 babies were born to mothers who had taken the drug, and of those 10,000 babies, over 40% died at birth.

And who developed this particular drug? - None other than the Nazi Heinrich Muckter, a high-ranking medical doctor, chemist and pharmacologist, who repeatedly experimented on concentration camp prisoners in Buchenwald, near Weimar in Germany. Not only did he manage to avoid prosecution for his crimes, but he also succeeded in becoming Head of Development in the German pharmaceutical company, Cherie Grunenthal, established by a man named Hermann Wirtz Sr., also a dedicated member of the Nazi eugenic programme. Also involved were Martin Staemmier, a medical doctor and also a proponent of the Nazi eugenic programmes, Heinz Baumkotter, chief medical officer at the Sachsenhausen concentration camps, located twenty-two miles north of Berlin, and last, but not least, Otto Ambroa, Hitler's very own adviser on chemical warfare. Ambroa was serving as chairman and member of the board of Grunenthal's advisory committee when Thalidomide was developed, and soon sold to the general public, first in West Germany and then worldwide.

When Mucker and others at Grunenthal were put on trial in Aachen in

Germany, in 1967, the company was indicted with intent to commit bodily harm and involuntary manslaughter, but despite the overwhelming evidence against them, criminal charges were mysteriously dropped, with Grunenthal agreeing to pay German thalidomide victims 31 million dollars in retributions.

But even though thalidomide was withdrawn in 1961, because of the birth defects and deaths, in 1998 it was approved in the United States as a treatment for cancer. Today it is available as a generic medicine, under the name 'Contergan' or 'Thalidomide'. And the WHO has it listed on its list of Essential Medicines!

So how can we have any kind of trust in our world health institutions when we know all of this?

And then of course we have the recent revelations about former Kwasi Kwarteng and again, - surprise, surprise! - Matt Hancock, agreeing to work for nothing less than £10,000 a day to further the interests of a fake South Korean firm after apparently being duped by the campaign group 'Led by Donkeys'. Caught red-handed serving their own financial interests!

The purported firm that approached the politicians did not exist and had a rudimentary foreign website with fake testimonials. MPs had been warned by the Home Office to be on their guard against the 'threat of foreign interference', and the group's investigation demonstrated the ease with which they seemed able to gain access to the MPs.

It said advisers would be required to attend six board meetings a year, with a 'very attractive' remuneration package and 'generous expenses' for international travel. Five MPs agreed to be interviewed on Zoom, with one who was clearly suspicious of the firm's credentials terminating the call. The MPs were interviewed by a woman purporting to be a senior executive, with a backdrop of the skyline of Seoul, the South Korean capital, at her office window.

In February, Kwarteng attended an online meeting of about 40 minutes, informing the interviewer that he was 'sitting in my office in parliament'. But Kwarteng was sacked as chancellor last October by the then prime minister Liz Truss after his mini-budget precipitated a financial crisis!

'Led By Donkeys' said it created a company called Hanseong Consulting, setting up a website which included made-up testimonials and paying for a so-called 'fake virtual office' in the South Korean capital Seoul. It said, after consulting the register of interests, that it approached 20 MPs from different parties asking if they would join the phoney firm's international advisory board. According to its preview video posted on social media, campaigners said 16 of the MPs contacted were Tory, two Labour, one Liberal Democrat and the other an independent. Five of those were said to have progressed to an online interview stage, including Hancock, Kwarteng, former defence secretary Sir Gavin Williamson, former minister Stephen Hammond and Sir Graham Brady, chairman of the Tories' 1922 Committee.

So what happened?

Kwasi Kwarteng told them that he might be able to set up a meeting with 'great guy' Boris Johnson. The former chancellor Kwarteng, and ex-health secretary Matt Hancock were both caught on camera offering to work for the firm for thousands of pounds per day. Kwarteng added that Johnson – who was then embroiled in the Partygate scandal – is the '*best campaigner you will ever see*'.

Kwarteng, the very same former chancellor, for a very brief period, in the equally brief premiership of Liz Truss, went on to suggest he could '*work with*' the firm's offer of paying him between £8,000 and £12,000 for each of the six annual meetings of its non-existent international advisory board. Kwarteng added that the Tory whips would allow him to attend board meetings for a foreign company. Asked about attending board meetings, he said: '*I could do that. I'm very flexible.......... We have whips ... but I can work with them to make sure that – as long as the meetings aren't like a whole week, I'm sure I can make that work.*'

Asked if he could also attend one-off meetings, he said*: 'I should be. I think you seem extremely professional and I would be very interested to see what you had to offer in this regard.*

I have a broad experience of business and finance ... I would say of my generation in the UK there are very few people who have had the breadth of experience that I've had across business and politics at the highest level, probably only two or three people.'

Hancock, also caught up in the '*Led By Donkeys*' sting, when asked whether he had a daily rate during an online '*interview*', said: '*I do, yes. It is 10,000 sterling.*'

And Kwarteng's asking fee? - '*I wouldn't do anything less than for about 10,000 dollars.....*'

Kwarteng, whose mini-budget in September sent the value of the pound tumbling and mortgage rates soaring, went on to clarify that he would prefer the rate to be in pound sterling.

Told by a fake employee of the company they were considering offering between £8,000 and £12,000 per day, with the intention for him to attend six board meetings a year, Kwarteng said: *'OK yes, we're not a million miles off. We can work with the numbers.'*

Is it any wonder that people's trust in government has been irretrievably lost?

And the police force! Current investigation into the Metropolitan Police Force has stated that the force is *'misogynist, homophobic'* and *'corrupt and rotten to the core.'* And we have certainly seen this just recently with all the crimes committed by serving police officers! No need for any further comment!

And of course the banking system! No need for any further comment here either!

Conspiracy theories! They are everywhere! This term, *'conspiracy theory'* originated after President J.F. Kennedy was assassinated, and the CIA were trying to cover-up what really happened, coining the term *'conspiracy theory'*. And ever since then anything that does not agree with the *'official'* version of whatever has happened, is designated as a *'conspiracy theory',* a derogatory term meant to devalue it as total fantasy, absurdity, imagination, annihilating its credibility. And all this when it was the American Government's own Warren Commission, which established and declared *'the lone gunman'* theory about Kennedy's assassination, - it was this very same Warren Commission that turned out to be the original conspiracy theorist! A cover-up!

Disinformation! A typical example of how, when you are in danger of being found out, go on the attack and accuse your accuser of doing what you have done!

Sleaze, sleaze and more sleaze! That's what our governments and our politicians have become. And when elections draw near, we are promised the usual, - a clean up of the sleaze, along with transparency and accountability. But it never happens! It still remains the same old, the same old, the same old. It's just the faces that change! And to say, as they constantly do, that they understand the problems the rest of us are facing, - well, how can they? They in their ivory towers, not plugged into the real world! Millionaires and billionaires, - how can they understand the needs and the problems of the majority of people? And just a change of faces is not the answer!

And the latest on the Nicola Sturgeon scandal? - That's anyone's guess! But her abrupt and sudden unexplained resignation? Well, like everything else hidden, it too is being revealed!

It's the system that needs to change! The system of government! And why? Simply because the present system is damaged beyond repair. It is just not viable to fill in the potholes or to bolster up a tumbling structure any longer. When the foundations are no longer sustaining the edifice, then the whole building needs to be lowered to the ground and rebuilt again from the start.

And when trust has been lost, - as our trust in our governments and politicians has been lost, then it is simply not possible to get that trust back!

The game of politics! That's what it is! - A game! And a dirty game! And the name of this game? - It's called *'feathering your own nest'* and *'looking after number one'.*

Indeed, politicians seem to have forgotten that they are the servants of the people, and not the other way round!

Deliberately induced mass global hysteria, fuelled by fear! That's what the world has just recently experienced! And it will not be the last time!

Unless we all WAKE UP! - NOW!

Chapter 6:

Who really rules the world?

We could well be forgiven for believing that our democratically elected politicians and world leaders rule the world. But how wrong can we be? - Very wrong!

President Woodrow Wilson stated:

'....there is a power so organised, so subtle, so complete, so pervasive, that they had better not speak above their breath when they speak in condemnation of it.'

And Felix Frankfurter, who served as U.S. Supreme Court Justice 1939-1962 stated:

'The real rulers in Washington are invisible and exercise power from behind the scenes.'

The big corporate paymasters at the top of the pyramid are the ones pulling the strings. The pyramid structure! That global system of power! A peaceful world is of no use to the big weapons and armaments industries! The big military-industrial complex, which wields so much power in our world! The secret government within the government!

In his farewell speech as president to the American people, President Eisenhower spoke about the dangers to society posed by this same military-industrial complex, the *'sham'* governments, and gave a clear warning about the growing power of the armaments industry to successfully lobby the US Congress for favourable policies:

'In the councils of government, we must guard against the acquisition of unwarranted influence, whether sought or unsought, by the military-industrial complex. The potential for the disastrous rise of misplaced power exists and will persist. We must never let the weight of this combination endanger our liberties or democratic processes. We should take nothing for granted. Only an alert and knowledgeable citizenry can compel the proper meshing of the huge industrial and military machinery of defense with our peaceful methods and goals, so that security and liberty may prosper together.'

Exactly what we are facing today! Eisenhower knew there were other forces than himself, - non-elected representatives, in control of what was happening. It is not our governments that have the power! It only seems that way. It seems like we live in a democracy, our politicians freely elected by us in a democratic process. And it seems those same government ministers are the ones who decide what happens on a daily basis on the national, the international and the world stage. That's what it seems! But *'nothing is what it seems'*! As I explained in my previous book. *'**Puppets on a string!'**,* presidents are SELECTED, not ELECTED!

And the economy? Ironically, war always boosts an economy! War industries are thriving, booming, all geared towards supporting and supplying the war effort! It's after the war that the bust sets in!

And this industrial boom during war time, along with the money made by the big armaments and weapons industries, - this explains why we are still such a warring world, even though 99 percent of the world's population want peace and an end to war. It's all about money!

And remember! It is the same weapons industries, whether they are

American, British, German, whatever, - the same arms manufacturers are selling to both sides! How's that for patriotism?

It's all about money! And when it's all about money, human lives are dispensable! War is BIG business! War is BIG money! And to those who are making that money, the COST in human lives is irrelevant!

And you might think events just happen, by chance or coincidence, and as they happen, humanity responds. Not true! Apart from there being no such thing as chance or coincidental happenings, absolutely everything being subject to the great Universal Law of Cause and Effect, there is, and always has been right down through history, a great plan, a great agenda. History has shown that there has always been someone, or a group of people intent on dominating humanity. And along with the planned agenda of the domination of humanity goes restriction of individual freedoms. In the words of Mussolini:

'The more complicated the forms of civilisation, the more restricted the freedom of the individual must become.'

And in the words of Denis Healey, UK Secretary of State for Defense 1964-1970, Deputy Leader of the Labour Party 1980-1983 and member of the secretive Elite-run and controlled Bilderberg group who are in effect the real world political policy-makers:

'World events do not occur by accident. They are made to happen, whether it is to do with national issues or commerce, and most of them are staged and managed by those who hold the purse strings.'

Those who hold the purse strings! The big bankers! And the biggest bankers of all? The Rockefellers and the Rothschilds!

Nathan Mayer Amschel Rothschild, speaking as early as 1790 said:

'Give me control of a nation's money and I care not who makes its laws.'

And in 1815:

'I care not what puppet is placed upon the throne of England to rule the Empire on which the sun never sets. The man who controls Britain's money supply controls the British Empire and I control the British money supply.'

Josiah Charles Stamp, 1st Baron Stamp, (1880-1941) was an English industrialist, economist, civil servant, statistician, writer, and banker. Director and Chairman of the Bank of England and Chairman of the London, Midland and Scottish Railway, he was the second richest man in Britain in the 1920s. He supported the *'appeasement* policy*'* towards Hitler, wrote articles for Herman Goering's magazine '*Der Vierjahresplan*' (the Four-Year Plan), and also attended the Nuremberg Party Rally as Hitler's guest. Stamp wrote:

'The modern banking system manufactures money out of nothing. The process is perhaps the most astounding piece of sleight of hand that was ever invented. Banking was conceived in inequity and born in sin....Bankers own the earth. Take it away from them but leave them the power to create money and, with a flick of a pen, they will create enough money to put it back again....Take this great power away from them and all great fortunes like mine will disappear, for then this would be a better and happier world to live in...But, if you want to continue to be the slaves of bankers and pay the cost of your own slavery, then let bankers continue to create money and control credit.'

Thomas Jefferson, the third president of the United States, 1801-1809 and a principal author of the Declaration of Independence wrote:

'I sincerely believe that banking institutions are more dangerous than standing armies. If the American people ever allow private banks to control the issue of their money, first by inflation and then by deflation, the banks and corporations that grow up around the banks, will deprive the people of their property until one day their children will wake up homeless on the continent their fathers conquered.'

And James Madison, who succeeded Thomas Jefferson as the fourth president of the United States, 1809-1817, and who played a pivotal role in drafting and promoting the Constitution of the United States and the United States Bill of Rights, wrote:

'History records that the money-changers (bankers) have used every form of abuse, intrigue, deceit, and violent means possible to maintain their control over governments by controlling money and its issuance.'

In other words, governments are controlled, held to ransom by the big banking institutions! The big banking institutions that are there to make money!

And what is the Trilateral Commission? The Trilateral Commission, along with the Council of Foreign Relations, was founded by none other than yours truly, David Rockefeller himself! These organisations get together to discuss foreign policy and ultimately are responsible for deciding the future of the world. United States Senator Barry Goldwater in his book *'With No Apologies'* wrote:

'The Trilateral Commission represents a skilful coordinated effort to seize control and consolidate the four centres of power - political, monetary, intellectual and ecclesiastical. What the Trilateral Commission intends is to create a worldwide economic power superior to the political governments of the nationstates involved. As managers

and creators of the system, they will rule the future.'

Please note! And I repeat:

'.........to create a worldwide economic power superior to the political governments of the nationstates involved.'

There we have it again! The long-term goal of the elite is the New World Order, and inherent in that New World Order is the development of a One World Economy, run by a One World Government, with a One World Religion. The global agenda!

Co-founder of the Trilateral Commission, Zbigniew Brzezinski, in his 1970 *'Between Two Ages'*, wrote:

'In the absence of social consensus society's emotional and rational needs may be fused......mass media makes this easier to achieve.....in the person of an individual who is seen as ......making the necessary innovations in the social order.'

And he continues:

'Such a society would be dominated by an elite whose claim to political power would rest on allegedly superior scientific know-how. Unhindered by the restraints of traditional liberal values, this elite would not hesitate to achieve its political ends by the latest modern techniques for the influencing public behavior and keeping society under close surveillance and control.'

And:

'Though Stalinism may have been a needless tragedy for both the Russian people and communism as an ideal, there is the intellectually

tantalizing possibility that for the world at large it was, as we shall see, a blessing in disguise.'

And Rockefeller after his 1973 visit to the People's Republic of China stated:

'The social experiment of China under Chairman Mao's leadership is one of the most important and successful in human history'.

Speaking at a United Nations Business Conference on 14th September 1994, this very same David Rockefeller said:

'We are on the verge of a global transformation. All we need is the right major crisis and the nations will accept the New World Order.'

Please note those words! *'All we need is the right major crisis'*! Remember! We have just seen that nothing happens by chance or coincidence, because there is no such thing! No *'major crisis'* just occurs! It is planned! Always!

'The right major crisis'! Like a world war? Like a world-wide pandemic? Like a global lock-down?

And in Rockefeller's book *'Memoirs'*:

'Some even believe we are part of a secret cabal working against the best interests of the United States, - characterizing my family and me as internationalists and of conspiring with others around the world to build a more integrated global political and economic structure: one world, if you will. If that's the charge, I stand guilty, and I am proud of it.'

Written in plain English! The agenda of a New World Order! One World Government! And if not by consent, then by conquest!

And President J.F. Kennedy knew it! Just seven days before his assassination he said:

'There's a plot in this country to enslave every man, woman and child. Before I leave this high and noble office, I intend to expose this plot'.

But seven days later, he was dead! Assassinated! Got rid of by order! Why? Obviously because he was onto something, some plot which he was going to expose and oppose!

So this *'New World Order'* spoken about so openly and expressly, is NOT just a conspiracy theory! It is a real agenda! And it means globalisation, world domination! And the most frightening thing? If not by consent, then by conquest!

We are all aware, through our mainstream media outlets, of how Communist Chinese and Soviet Russian governments are able to fool their citizens into believing that they live in some sort of social paradise, a utopia, while we here in Western Society live in a blissful state of democratic freedom. And we have pity and compassion for them, but the truth is, for those who want to see it, that our Western history is every bit as distorted, controlled and censored just as much as it was in Nazi Germany, and is, in Communist China and Communist Russia! Our so-called *'news'* and *'history'*, - they are all a form of propaganda, no less than in China or Russia, all intended to control our thinking, and steer us to adhering to a particular planned agenda, through social engineering. We are told how to live, what to think, what to say, what to do and what we can know or not know.

And we think we live in a democratic state? To quote Thomas Jefferson again, the third president of the United States, 1801-1809 and a principal author of the Declaration of Independence:

'*Democracy is two wolves and a sheep voting on what to have for dinner. Liberty is a well-armed lamb contesting the vote.*'

And this move towards a New World Order, towards world domination, - a conspiracy theory IT IS NOT! It is a real agenda! An open agenda! An '*Open Conspiracy*' even! Henry Kissinger talked about his '*New World Order*'. George Soros left the World Economic Forum in Davos proclaiming:

'*The 2020 US election will determine the fate of the whole world*'.

Joe Biden has said:

'*The affirmative task we have now is to create a new world order.*'

Klaus Schwab, founder of the World Economic Forum, usually meeting in Davos said:

'*The world must act jointly and swiftly to revamp all aspects of our societies and economies, from education to social contracts and working conditions. Every country, from the United States to China, must participate, and every industry, from oil and gas to tech must be transformed.*'

And speaking at a mass rally of several million people in Berlin on Saturday, 29th August 2020, Robert Kennedy Junior said:

'*Governments love pandemics. They love pandemics for the same reason they love war. Because it gives them the ability to impose controls on the population that the population would otherwise never accept. To create institutions and mechanisms for orchestrating and imposing obedience.*'

A New World Order! The Roman emperors tried it, as did Napoleon, Hitler and many others like them, all aspiring in that direction! And although none of them ever actually succeeded in the long term, they sure unleashed untold pain and suffering upon humanity in the process of each and every attempt!

And in pursuit of this world domination, what is necessary? In the words of Dr. George Brock Chisholm, who served as the first Director-General of the World Health Organisation (WHO) from 1948 to 1953:

'To achieve world government, it is necessary to remove from the minds of men their individualism, loyalty to family tradition, national patriotism and religious dogmas.'

George Chisholm here echoing the words spoken previously by David Rockefeller, in his address to the meeting of the Trilateral Commission in June 1991:

'The supranational sovereignty of an intellectual elite and world bankers is surely preferable to the national auto determination practised in past centuries.'

Chester Ward was Judge Advocate General of the U.S. Navy in the 1950s, the highest-ranking uniformed lawyer in the US Department of the Navy, principal advisor to the Secretary of the Navy and the Chief of Naval operations on legal matters pertaining to the Navy. He was also a former member of the Council on Foreign Relations for over 16 years. However, he explained his disapproval of the Council, calling it a *'shadow government'*:

'The most powerful clique in these elitist groups have one objective in common: they want to bring about the surrender of the sovereignty of

the national independence of the United States. A second clique of international members of the CFR comprises Wall Street international bankers and their key agents. Primarily, they want the world banking monopoly from whatever power ends up in the control of global government.....Once the ruling members of the CFR shadow government have decided that the U.S. Government should adopt a particular policy the very substantial research facilities of CFR are put to work to develop arguments intellectual and emotional to support the new policy and to confound and discredit intellectually and politically any opposition. The main purpose of the Council on Foreign Relations is promoting the disarmament of U.S. sovereignty and national independence and submerge into an all powerful one world government.'

Georgetown University professor, historian and political theorist Carroll Quigley, in his 1966 book *'Tragedy and Hope'* wrote:

'The CFR is the American Branch of a society which originated in England, and which believes that national boundaries should be obliterated, and a one-world rule established'.

And former FBI agent Dan Smoot, in his book *'The Invisible Government'*, specifically referred to the CFR:

'The ultimate aim of the CFR is to create a one-world socialist system, and to make the U.S. an official part of it'.

In his book, *'The World's Most Dangerous Secret Societies'* author James Jackson explores the hidden agenda and the ultimate goal of a New World Order and world domination. He poses the questions, could it be that there walks among us, in any given echelon of the population, groups given to exercise inordinate amounts of power and influence over the rest of us? And, could these exotic members-only clubs really pose such an immediate threat to our well-being that our very way of life is endangered? In response to these questions, Jackson writes:

'Quite frankly, the disturbing answer to those particular questions are yes and yes. Right in our midst there absolutely exists clandestine organizations consisting of both men and women who wield a dangerous amount of influence and power over the entire populace.'

So too Jackson warns about the dangers posed by the Council on Foreign Relations:

'.........the Council on Foreign Relations represents one thread in a many tangled web of entities that seek the creation of a centralized world economic super-power, ruled neither by the democratic interests of its citizens nor their democratically-elected leaders, but by an international conglomerate of industry moguls, media figureheads, transnational corporations and elected global political leaders who seek absolute authority and absolute control over the exchange of finance, media and thought. To this end, key Council initiatives, such as the implementation of NAFTA (North Atlantic Free Trade Agreement) under Council member and then-President Bill Clinton (which benefited only those corporations large enough to buy into intercontinental trade and subjected three separate nations to a totalitarian restriction of economic Social Darwinism in practice) and the European Union (itself a product of Bilderberg architect Jozef Retinger) were established, lulling millions of Americans into a pipe-dream of greater material prosperity and alleged 'security' while all the while tightening its grip around their collective throat. The danger of the Council is that so many citizens refuse to acknowledge it as anything more than an established pattern in the American fabric of life.' ('The World's Most Dangerous Secret Societies', James Jackson)

Amongst the list of members of this Council on Foreign Relations, Jackson includes: Former Director of U.S. Policy Planning Richard Haas; Federal Reserve Bank President Michael Moskow; former U.S. Ambassadors Morris Abramowitz, Walter Roberts and George Kennan; media mogul Oprah Winfrey; National Security Advisor Stewart Baker; 9/11 Commission Chairman Thomas Kean; Senators Sam Nunn, Jay Rockefeller and Joseph Lieberman; Fox Media CEO Rupert Murdock; Former Vice Presidents Gerald Ford, Dick Cheney and Al Gore; former CIA Directors Allen Dulles and General David Petraeus; media pundit William F. Buckley; former Foreign Affairs Advisor William Bundy; Joint Chief of Staff Chairman Colin Powell; billionaire investor George Soros; Former Secretaries of State Warren Christopher, Madeleine Albright and Condoleeza Rice; ABC Television CEO Thomas Murphy; Television news anchors Tom Brokaw, Bill Moyers and Barbara Walters; Former New Jersey State Governor Christine Todd Whitman; Coca-Cola CEO Muhtar Kent; Boeing CEO Donna Hrinak; Disney President Michael Ovitz; - and the list goes on! An impressive elitist list indeed!

So, - an end to individual national sovereignty is a necessary pre-requisite on the road to world domination! And in this light, have you ever wondered about the massive refugee crisis across the entire world lately? Let us remind ourselves again of what President Franklin D. Roosevelt said:

'In politics, nothing happens by accident. If it happens, you can bet it was planned that way.'

'You can bet it was planned that way.' - A planned, an organised, a deliberately manufactured refugee crisis? By the only ones who could possibly bring it all about, - the holders of the biggest purse strings! Why? To break up individual national sovereignty! To infiltrate every

country in the world with refugees! To break down national identity! To destroy national cohesiveness! All a vital part of their agenda of world domination! An agenda that requires a total breakdown of existing institutions!

Those 'who hold the purse strings'! The Rockefellers and their cohorts! These are the ones who control our world and dictate our lives! And you thought it was our elected governments? The famed author H. G. Wells in his 1928 book, 'The Open Conspiracy' wrote:

'Not only are the present governments of the world a fragmentary competitive confusion, but none of them is as simple as it appears. They seem to be simple because they have formal heads and definite forms, councils, voting assemblies, and so forth, for arriving at decisions. But the formal heads, the kings, presidents, and so forth, are really not the directive heads. They are merely the figure heads. They do not decide. They merely make gestures of potent and dignified acquiescence when decisions are put to them. They are complicating shams. Nor do the councils and assemblies really decide. They record, often very imperfectly and exasperatingly, the accumulating purpose of outer forces. These outer really directive forces are no doubt very intricate in their operation; they depend finally on religious and educational forms and upon waves of gregarious feeling, but it does not in the least simplify the process of collective human activity to pretend that it is simple and to set up symbols and dummies in the guise of rulers and dictators to embody that pretense.'

Please note those words, - 'They depend on religious and educational forms'!

That means that religion and education are the chief methods, apart from the media of course, through which social engineering is achieved!

William Melvin Hicks (1961-1994) was an American stand-up comedian, social critic and musician. His material encompassed a wide range of social issues including religion, politics and philosophy. On his premature death from cancer in 1995, the *'Montreal Gazette'* referred to him as one of the greatest comedians who ever lived, in the opinions of those who saw him.

In one of his acts, Hicks told his audience:

'I have this feeling man, cos you know there's a handful of people actually run everything. That's true, it's provable. A handful, a very small elite group run and own these corporations, which include the mainstream media. I have this feeling whoever's elected President, ...no matter what you promise on the campaign trail, 'blah, blah, blah', when you win, you go into this smoky room in the basement of the White House with the twelve industrialist, capitalist scum-f**ks who got you in there and you're in this smoky room and the little screen comes down and a big guy with a cigar says, 'roll the film'. And it's a shot of the Kennedy assassination from an angle you've never seen before.....that looks suspiciously off the grassy knoll. And then the film ends, the screen goes up and the lights come on and they say to the new guy, 'Any questions Mr. President?' (Quoted in *'The Falsification of History'*, John Hamer, page 38)

Quoting Thomas Jefferson again:

'Democracy is two wolves and a sheep voting on what to have for dinner. Liberty is a well-armed lamb contesting the vote.'

And Bill Clinton:

'*There is a government inside the government'.*

A parallel and unseen government that runs all the institutions and companies! A parallel and unseen government that works behind the scenes of our supposedly democratically elected politicians and global financiers we see in the news and on mainstream media.

The movie '*V for Vendetta', came* out in 2005 and is about a totalitarian dictatorship that gains its power by creating a society of fear due to an alleged virus spreading throughout the world. In the film the media pushes fear-based propaganda on the television screen of every household and in the city's streets. The authoritarian dictator promises security but not freedom. The constant theme of '*This is for your safety*' is repeated throughout the whole film. Most importantly, the movie ends with society waking up and the corrupt, fascist regime is dismantled. Guess what year the film is set? 2020!

Fear! The most negative of energies in all of creation! The paralysis that fear creates! It is fear that enables control to creep into society. In the words of U.S. President Harry Truman:

'*When even one American who has done nothing wrong is forced by fear to shut his mind and close his mouth, then all Americans are in peril.*'

And pay attention to the words of Bill Gates:

'*You don't have a choice...the world's population will be vaccinated.*'

And!

'*This is not a vaccine story. This is a population management story.*'

Bill Gates! Non-elected! But self-proclaimed expert on health matters -

despite the fact that he has no medical training whatsoever! Founder of Microsoft! Complete power and control over WHO! WHO will do as Gates says! And why? Because he has money! One of the richest, if not actually the richest man in the world! He who believes all health problems can be solved through a syringe!

So! Our world as we know it! A world not controlled by our elected representatives! But by self-appointed controllers and others selected because they will maintain and sustain the status quo!

Now imagine a world where these greedy power-hungry monsters no longer exist! Imagine a world where these greatly and deliberately deceiving and instilled beliefs are rectified, changed, abandoned; a world where our actions change as a result of these beliefs being abandoned. What sort of world would that be?

That would be a world where everyone would have enough to eat, where everyone would have clean water, where everyone would have a safe place to call home, where everyone would have access to an informative and freeing education system, and to a system of health care. Simply because we would see ourselves as all One.

What a wonderful world that would be!

BUT! That can only ever happen when we all WAKE UP!

Chapter 7:

Programming and conditioning

From the moment we are born we are being programmed and conditioned! But for what?

To fit into the system! To maintain the status quo! Victims of mass propaganda! Victims of mind-control! Very subtly done! So subtly that we do not even notice!

And what does the system do? It turns people into machines! Into robots! Into non-thinking automatics! Into zombies!

Remember the words of Hitler? -

'What good fortune for governments that the people do not think.'

We have become entrapped, ironically, in what we think is freedom! Trapped by television, cell phones, computers, the Internet, all electronic screens and of course gaming programmes.

Most people in actual fact are now addicted! Bound to the techno-grid! Plugged into the technology trap! Trapped in the continuing cycle of hypnosis-inducing technology! Dictated to by programming! Controlled by radiation-producing, addictive devices!

Television and all the other electronic devices that dominate our world and our lives are not here just to entertain us, as we tend to think, but to entrap us! Designed by Big Tech to enslave us, through a sophisticated method of mind control! We are being targeted by television, computers, cell phones and all other electronic screens to take us into a hypnotic trance state within seconds, without us ever even being aware of how we are being entrapped by the energy frequencies used against us by these devices. Our nervous system is being manipulated by pulsing images displayed on the screen in front of us, our subconscious receiving and absorbing what those who control us want us to think, to want, and of course to fear. Hence they are called 'programmes'. Simply because they are 'programming' us. Programming us with electro-magnetic programming! And we don't even know it! Yes, television connects us to the world, and with all sorts of useful information in every conceivable field, but the main function of television now is to act as a powerful tool for spreading propaganda through the use of mind control!

And computer software has now become far more invasive! We have been caught off-guard! We have allowed these devices to take over our lives, making us the slave rather than the master. Most people are now spending more than half of their waking, conscious hours glued to an addictive device! Completely unaware that all this technology has been deliberately designed to alter the mind electronically, through persuasive programming.

The cell phone, the television and the computer are all designed to be more addictive than any available substance on earth. Television! - The dominant means of information and news for the last number of generations! Television! - The all-encompassing drug par excellence! Television! - The tool used by the large media companies to coerce, brainwash, manipulate and control the masses! Those same large media companies that in turn are owned and managed by the powerful elite ruling- class families, all intent on suppressing human consciousness, keeping us in total submission to their agenda! All those so-called *'reality'* television shows! And we continue to watch, becoming hooked on following other people's frivolous and false lives, - all stage-managed and falsified for the television camera, for television viewers.

We are fed a constant diet of violence, violence and more violence! Scenarios set up to deliberately create confrontations, chat shows with controversy to the fore, news programmes that bring us nothing but negativity, negativity, negativity! And we think all of this is our world! We are constantly viewing ourselves killing each other, hating each other, fearing each other! And so we keep the cycle going, - killing, hating, fearing. And all because we are constantly being exposed to all this in the electronic devices that have taken over our lives!

In fact, we have now become not just hooked or addicted, but dependent on them! Dependent on them for our banking, running our businesses, sourcing our information and even with the satnav in our cars directing us and guiding us to where we want to go! Not to mention Alexa! Big Brother in operation! All and any information immediately relayed! Its real purpose is to spy on us and record us in the privacy of our own homes! And all fed into a central computer, into a central AI system.

Are we moving rapidly toward the Big Brother system already well established in China? A system that monitors every deed and spoken word with all behaviours fed into the AI system that determines your social rating, and rewarding or punishing you accordingly?

And what about our children? Constantly being overexposed to all this technology leads to addiction, social isolation, lethargy, intellectual, physical and emotional lock-down. Obesity, lack of fitness, nervous and mental disorders, depression and withdrawal from society are all becoming more prevalent in children who are sitting in front of a screen or so many hours each day of their young lives.

Television! It permeates everywhere! Tentacles all over the place! The advertising that makes us feel we are incomplete, and we will not be complete until we buy into these material goods, that promise a false world. The constant violence and the false portrayal of life, - all making us believe that this is the real world in which we live. All manipulating and brainwashing us in a dangerous, negative way.

Daniel Estulin, author of *'Tavistock Institute: Social Engineering the Masses',* writes:

'The biggest hypnotist in the world is an oblong box in the corner of the room that tells people what to believe. Television, with its reach into everyone's home, creates the basis for the mass brainwashing of citizens.......... your television works as a high-tech drug delivery system, and we all feel its effects.......For the brainwashers in charge of this societal transformation, they have pulled off the ultimate trick. They were able to persuade people that what they can see with their eyes is what's there to see. Subsequently, people will laugh in your face when you try to explain to them the bigger picture and the unseen reality behind the curtain......

In a 1981 interview, Hal Becker from a think-tank called 'Futures Group' in Connecticut said: 'I know the secret of making the average American believe anything I want him to. Just let me control television......You put something on the television and it becomes reality. If the world outside the TV set contradicts the images, people start trying to change the world to make it like the TV set images......You see, television is not the truth, for as much as people keep tuning in to its lies. Television is an amusement park ....huge numbers of people at the top are prepared to tell you anything in the name of 'war against terror', audience share and advertising dollars as long as you vote for them, buy their products and allow them to create an homogenous culture, a mass culture, through which popular opinion could be shaped and controlled, so that everyone in the country would think the same.......Why is it being done? To dumb you down. To brainwash you. To turn you into a touchy-feely adult with infantile tendencies. So you don't get in the way of important people by doing too much thinking on your own.' (Daniel Estulin, *'Tavistock Institute'* page 123-124)

As Oscar Wilde wrote:

'Most people are other people. Their thoughts are someone else's opinions, their lives a mimicry, their passions a quotation.'

And the idea of a large organisation controlling the minds and thoughts of every individual, steering and forcing them towards certain actions and beliefs, may indeed seem as science fiction, or as an absurd conspiracy found only in books and movies. But the CIA controlling and manipulating civilians' minds is not fiction. It was a fact in the United States in the last century, and it is still a fact today, and not just in the United States.

President Kennedy knew it. In December 1960, in the Waldorf-Astoria Hotel in New York, Kennedy addressed the American Newspaper Publishers Association in a famous speech, entitled *'The President and the Press'*:

'We decided long ago that the dangers of excessive and unwarranted concealment of pertinent facts far outweigh the dangers which are cited

to justify it. Even today, there is little value in opposing the threat of a closed society by imitating its arbitrary restrictions. Even today, there is little value in insuring the survival of our nation if our traditions do not survive with it. And there is very grave danger that an announced need for increased security will be seized upon by those anxious to expand its meaning to the very limits of official censorship and concealment. That, I do not intend to permit to the extent that it is in my control. And no official of my Administration, whether his rank is high, or low, civilian or military, should interpret my words here tonight as an excuse to censor the news, to stifle dissent, to cover up our mistake or to withhold from the press and the public the facts that they deserve to know.'

David Sedgwick's first book, '*BBC: Brainwashing Britain*', is a shocking exposure of mass propaganda, explaining how the people of Britain are under attack, being brainwashed completely, ceaselessly and cynically. Sedgwick reveals in his book the many tricks and subterfuges used by the BBC, for example, to wilfully, deceitfully and incessantly brainwash us, controlling our minds and determining our actions.

'The BBC frequently leads the national debate. Its 6 o'clock and 10 o'clock news bulletins can promote a given topic to such an extent it becomes an instant talking point not only amongst suburban housewives in Surrey, but among cabinet ministers too. BBC talking points can be instantly disseminated around the world via its .co.uk and .com portals - websites regularly ranked inside the world's top 100 in terms of footfall. This is a serious level of influence.' (David Sedgwick, '*BBC: Brainwashing Britain*' page 6-7)

Cell phones! The must-have gadget! But! - Big Brother's ultimate and primary control mechanism! And as they continue to get more sophisticated and advanced, Big Tech is ramping up the radiation and the electromagnetic pulse! Every single move we make is being tracked, with someone somewhere listening, screening and storing your voice and conversations. Like an eternal school-yard bully, - stalking, hounding, following you all the time!

And of course, to understand how great a controlling mechanism the cell phone really is, you just have to think of what was going on during the recent 'pandemic'! How the cell phone was used to trace your movements, where you were at any given time, were you obeying the isolation rules, or were you out and about defying these rules?

Computers! How could we possibly ever have lived without them? And certainly during the recent 'pandemic'! But at what cost? How much radiation are we actually absorbing as we constantly stare into the screen? How much damage are we doing to our eyes? And to our energy field?

Gaming! The ultimate in entertainment! High tech! But! - High level mind control! And much more addictive than most illicit drugs! Sucking the life force out of you! Manipulating you! Isolating you! Trapping you in a simulated world, where every outcome in the game that you can possibly come up with is already included within the simulated reality programme!

And so we now find ourselves in our present situation, where the media is being used to propel us all into a certain way of thinking and acting! Brad Martin and Mike Smith, both Hollywood stunt co-ordinators and action directors, and who featured in the recent documentary, 'Out of Shadows', both maintain that the connection between the United States government personnel and media corporations is 'unbelievable'.

Google, Amazon, Twitter, Netflix. CNN, NBC - they all have the same protocol and agenda. We believe that people in the media and to whom we are listening have our best interests in mind, but they do not! They can place any agenda on people that they choose.

There is no doubt the press is corrupt to its core. Its agenda is making money, under the direction of corporate chieftains, not delivering truth to its readership. The truth has gone! And how do they make their money? By going after a certain segment and running wild with it, to the point of extreme sensationalism. Playing to the audience! For example, smashing Trump or smashing Johnson, or whoever, is good for business. So that's what they do. They build people up in order to bring them down! They create stories. They mess with people's lives. And to them, everyone is fair game!

And the fake news, the lies, the propaganda did not start just yesterday or yesteryear! Oh no! That has all been going on right down through history!

Mainstream media! The front for it all! Those who really pull the strings remaining out of *'the bright lights of publicity',* operating behind the scenes.

Edmund Sixtus Muskie 1914-1996 was an American statesman and political leader who served as the 58th United States Secretary of State under President Jimmy Carter, as United States Senator from Maine from 1959 to 1980, as the 64th Governor of Maine from 1955 to 1959, and as a member of the Maine House of Representatives from 1946 to 1951. In Muskie's words:

'Looking at yourself through the media is like looking at one of those rippled mirrors in an amusement park.'

BBC plays a vital role in protecting those at the top, the *'dominant minority',* those who pull the strings! This explains how BBC interviews with individuals of whom it approves are conducted in an entirely different way from those of whom it disapproves. Certain politicians can get away with saying the same things as other politicians are attacked for saying. Some news is given prolific coverage while other news is ignored completely. And it is the mainstream media, controlled by the big corporations, the big bankers, those at the top of the pyramid, who facilitate the world-wide agenda that these puppeteers command and demand.

David Rockefeller, founder of the Trilateral Commission, in an address to a meeting of The Trilateral Commission in June 1991 said:

'We are grateful to The Washington Post, the New York Times, Time Magazine and other great publications whose directors have attended our meetings and respected their promises of discretion for almost forty years. It would have been impossible for us to develop our plan for the world if we had been subject to the bright lights of publicity during those years. But, the work is now much more sophisticated and prepared to march towards a world government. The supranational sovereignty of an intellectual elite and world bankers is surely preferable to the national auto determination practised in past centuries.'

The power and efficacy of the mainstream media! Acknowledged by none other than David Rockefeller himself! He who pulls their strings! He whose agenda they push forward!

And of course, we cannot neglect to mention what must surely be one of the greatest scandals of the BBC and the shock people felt when it was disclosed - BBC's Pudsey Bear, the mascot for their *'Children In*

Need' annual appeal for money! A total mockery of BBC viewers, arrogantly exploiting their generosity and kindness by covering up the real truth behind Pudsey. And what is the truth?

An organisation which covered up so much paedophilia, pulling on the heart strings of viewers to help alleviate the hardships suffered by so many children, while at the same time, it was BBC celebrities who were abusing children and the BBC itself covering up for them! Unsuspecting viewers persuaded to contribute generously by the friendly, smooth-talking, affable Terry Wogan. Rolf Harris, Gary Glitter, Jimmy Savile, all known paedophiles, all appeared on *'Children In Need'* clutching Pudsey Bear and imploring the public to donate generously. And the vast amounts of money raised? The bulk went to paying executive salaries and *'administration'* costs. In 2013, the BBC-supported *'Comic Relief'* was found to have invested in tobacco and arms companies. The findings were even reported on an episode of BBC's own *'Panorama'* - BBC distancing itself from the scandal! And Lenny Henry, the friendly, smooth-talking, affable host of *'Comic Relief'* for many years, was made a Knight Bachelor in the Queen's Birthday Honours in 2015. How ironic and cynical is that!

And *'Children In Need'*? Would that be more appropriately read as *'in need of children',* bearing in mind what we now know was really going on?

Let us not be hoodwinked any longer! Let us be aware of what is going on in the media, how we are being manipulated and herded like sheep or cattle! Let us cease to be divided and ruled! Do what is in your own heart! Because your contribution to humanity is a unique contribution! You have a song to sing, YOUR song, and you have a right to sing your song, to sound your own unique note, contributing to the one Great

Cosmic Orchestra, the one Great Universal Harmony.

Do not allow the mockingbird to be killed within your beautiful soul! The voice within you has a right to be heard! And no one has the right to deprive you of that!

And a final word! If you want to know what is going on in the world, don't read the newspapers or watch television news! Because the truth - well, you just ain't going to find it there! Words, phrases and sentences are inserted, switched around, meanings are changed, photographs are doctored, images are distorted, - these guys are experts at propaganda! Propaganda, collusion, fabrication! This is what they do! And that's what the mainstream media outlet network is! Propaganda! Spin! All fake news!

Propaganda! Fake news! Lies! Spin! What's the difference? - None!

And it's the same in Hollywood, in the music industry and in the fashion industry, as I explained in great detail in '***Puppets on a String***' published in 2020.

Hollywood! When we think of the entertainment industry, we immediately think of movies, and hence Hollywood! But have we ever stopped to question the content of what is coming out of Hollywood? What exactly are we watching? Have we ever considered that our governments might be controlling the content of what we are watching and hearing?

Nothing is ever as it seems! Oh no! - Fact! Sad but true! There is always the illusion and there is always the reality. There is always the surface and there is always what is happening underneath the surface.

Hollywood! Tinseltown! On the surface, - glitz, glamour, fame, fortune, awards, Oscars, the red carpet! The American Dream! But underneath the glaring facade of all this, there lurks a seedy, murky underworld, - a seedy murky underworld of corruption, casting couches, pedophilia, mafia, drug barons, and of course gruesome satanic practices!

Hollywood as a dark occult empire is well documented by Jay Dyer, whose work has focused on the interplay of film, geopolitics, espionage and psychological warfare. Dyer is a public speaker and lecturer, and the author of 'Esoteric Hollywood: Sex, Cults and Symbols in Film'. A title which is self-explanatory!

Dyer writes:

'The camera is much more than a recording apparatus; it is a medium via which messages reach us from another world that is not ours and that brings us to the heart of a great secret.' (Jay Dyer, 'Esoteric Hollywood' page 4)

The late Edward Bernays was a nephew of Sigmund Freud and famed for his works on propaganda and mass advertising. Bernays pioneered methods and techniques for influencing and altering mass opinion. He focused on crowd psychology and for a time worked for the United States government on originating the concept of public relations and the 'herd instinct'. Bernays wrote:

'The American motion picture is the greatest unconscious carrier of propaganda in the world today. It is a great distributor for ideas and opinions'. (Quoted in Jay Dyer, 'Esoteric Hollywood', page 99)

The films we watch, the movies we love, - they are not just for our entertainment, oh no! They are all made with a particular agenda, a particular purpose, all meant to have a particular effect on their audience. Every film, every movie we watch - they are all, each and every one, without exception, permeated with symbolism, all connected to politics, events in history, both past and present and yet to come, - remember those words of George Orwell, in his dystopian '1984': *'Who controls the past controls the future. Who controls the present controls the past',* - religion, social engineering, and manipulation, psychological warfare, esoteric dimensions and delving into the negative aspects of the occult. And you thought you were going out for a great fun night at the movies! Pop-corn and all that! Think again! Get away from the herd! Think for yourself!

WAKE UP!

Apparently, what is being filmed in Hollywood is happening in real life! Or it **will** happen! That's the message!

So to cut a long story short, are we being prepared in the films we are watching for the future we are going to experience? Dyer writes:

'Make no mistake about it, it is very real, very public, and very much an open tool of the globalists.' (Jay Dyer, 'Esoteric Hollywood', page 213)

And this goes all the way back to pre-1947, when United States Intelligence was using modern pictures to alter the thinking of people in America. Movies are a powerful propaganda weapon, a means of psychological warfare, as a project study showed:

'They can be aimed at the civilians and the armed forces of the United States, to inform and instruct, to create attitudes, to stimulate and inhibit action, to build morale.'

And video games! The video-game industry, a billion dollar industry in America, is no doubt a weapon for mass social control and brainwashing. Used after World War Two in the immediate post-war period, video games were training instruments for the military and law enforcement agencies. And we are now addicted to them! As Alexander Freeman, author, researcher and film-maker wrote:

'Culture has been usurped by mind-control.'

 And the music industry! No different from the film industry in that it too is under the control of the ruling elite. All used as propaganda, mind control and social engineering, influencing mass audiences to adopt a certain version of '*norm*'.

'The dark manipulations of the music industry are as old as the industry itself, and early examples of the dubious calling cards evident in the contemporary scene are equally present in its formative years. Mind-control, military 'intelligence', paedophilia and occult fascination are, it seems, nothing new.' (Mark Devlin '*Musical Truths*' page 17.)

The blatant use of individuals, building them up into celebrities, raising them to stardom, in order to have them influence an unsuspecting public, who will copy them. Subliminal messages everywhere surrounding these music artists, from the titles of their albums to symbols, to their programmed hand gestures!

And let us not forget the fashion industry! The more sinister subliminal mind-controlling that is going on underneath the surface!

The famous song '*Dedicated Followers of Fashion*' which has become a metaphor for slavish conformity, handing over of one's power to those who dictate what we should or should not wear. The blatant use of symbols that is becoming more blatant in the fashion industry, conveying a message, putting people under certain influences, - all of this I have explained in greater detail in **'Puppets On A String'** published in 2020.

Military-style clothes, leopard prints, cat imagery, Micky-Mouse ears, - all part of the agenda! An agenda hidden in our clothing!

And the cosmetic industry! Tattoos everywhere! All carrying subliminal messages! Not to mention the make-up industry! That's a whole story on its own!

The subtle programming that is going on! Take for example, the adverts on our television screens during the '*pandemic*', where Ryanair was telling us '*Vax and go!*'; Jet2 Holidays telling *us 'Get the jab and book your holiday and if your plans change, you can cancel our booking!'* and in '*Mrs Browns' Boys*' the '*dopey*' son, Buster, dressed in a plastic tube vaccination outfit, with the words '*Get the jab*' written all over it!

See the subtle programming going on? Ryanair and the holiday companies getting the message across to us, without specifically saying it, that we will not be able to travel unless we get vaccinated first! And mainstream media delivering the message!

So you still do not believe you are being constantly programmed and conditioned to someone else's agenda? Someone else's narrative?

YOU NEED TO WAKE UP!

Chapter 8:

DNA and the Pineal Gland

We are spiritual beings having a physical experience. We are all in a physical body here on this third dimension earth energy vibration level, our body being the organic vessel through which our consciousness experiences our physical reality. So as both spiritual and physical beings, our brain connects to higher states of energy and consciousness, as well as to all that is around us on this more dense third dimension.

There must, therefore, be some sort of a connecting point somewhere within our being, that enables us to connect with the higher energy forces, higher levels of consciousness, while still remaining in our physical body.

And yes, there is! And it is called the '*pineal gland*'!

Our brain and DNA are like computer terminals, receiving and transmitting data and information. The brain has two hemispheres, - the right and the left. The pineal gland is a pee-sized organ which is situated between these two hemispheres. This spot is also referred to as one of the chakras, known as the '*Third Eye*'. Since ancient times yogis have always given much importance to this spot between the two eyebrows. This is the place where they believe the soul resides.

The 17th century philosopher and scientist René Descartes in both his first book '*Treatise of Man*', and in his last book, '*The Passions of the Soul*' described the pineal gland as being '*the principal seat of the soul and the place in which all our thoughts are formed.*' In the '*Treatise of*

Man', he describes humans as creatures created by God, and having two ingredients, - a body and a soul. In the *'Passions of the Soul'*, he emphasised that the soul is joined to the whole body by *'a certain very small gland situated in the middle of the brain's substance and suspended above the passage through which the spirits in the brain's anterior cavities communicate with those in its posterior cavities.'* Descartes gave importance to this particular structure as it was the only unpaired component of the brain. Today, it is still referred to as being the seat of the Soul or the seat of Consciousness.

The knowledge of the pineal gland and the association with the so-called *'third eye'*, also known as the *'all-seeing eye'*, dates back to very ancient times and we can find so many representations in various cultures throughout human history. In fact this symbol of the *'all-seeing eye'* is everywhere! Even and especially on the dollar bill! And in numerous sacred temples around the world, - such as the Cai Dai Temple in Vietnam, where the altar in the prayer hall is known as the *'Altar of the Eye'*, - the *'all-seeing eye'*.

Pythagoras, Plato, Iamblichus and others wrote of this gland with great reverence. So we must surely want to ask why is the pineal gland represented so clearly in so many different places and cultures throughout history? What is its significance? Elusive and unique it certainly is!

From an esoteric or spiritual point of view, the pineal gland represents the mystical *'third eye'*, or the *'eye of the Soul'*, the eye that is able to see reality, which is not what appears to our limited physical eyes, but the more *'subtle'* one, hidden by the *'veil of maya'*. This third eye is able to *'see'* the invisible, to *'see'* beyond ordinary vision, to perceive the 95% of reality that our human eyes do not perceive, - our perception with our ordinary senses is severely limited to only about 5% of what actually exists out there.

This third eye, in the ancient Hindu and Buddhist tradition, corresponds with the sixth chakra, the Ajna, located at the center of the forehead between the eyebrows. This center represents the inner eye, able to perceive reality beyond the ordinary vision, it is the door of clairvoyance and of the superior vision. The third eye is the connection with one's intuitive mind, with the Higher Self, let us also say with one's Soul.

The pineal gland is responsible for your DNA system. It is capable of making a compound called DMT. DMT is released from the pineal gland during extraordinary states such as the time of death and the time of birth. So this gland may be the mechanism from which we enter and leave our physical bodies. This demonstrates the fact that DMT acts as a 'bridge' between the physical body and the spiritual world. And it is the pineal gland that produces it!

In some people, even during sleep, the pineal gland secretes a sufficient amount of DMT, which makes possible special experiences such as lucid dreams or astral travels.

This pineal gland is a source of the mystical dimension of our life. There are many mystical sides of this gland and that's why it becomes interesting to know more about it. Apart from our eye cells, even pineal gland cells are light-sensitive, hence the pineal gland is known to regulate our biological clock, since it can sense light and darkness and at night when you close your eyes, everything is dark and in that state, the pineal gland releases melatonin, which is a structurally simple hormone, and this hormone regulates our biological clock as it communicates information about environmental lighting to various parts of the body.

Melatonin is synthesized by two substances: tryptophan and serotonin. The latter is a neurotransmitter used in the regulation of body temperature, sense of hunger, satiety and mood. In fact, it is also nicknamed *'the hormone of happiness'.* So the pineal gland works in many mysterious ways and holds many mysteries.

The legendary Indian sage, Sage Vyas, taught that there is an invisible hole in this region between the two eyebrows, which is luminous and spreads light. It spreads coronal light and by focusing on this light, he said he could see beings between earth and the higher spaces, so it is believed that this gland connects the person to the higher world.

The contemporary Yoga tradition holds the *'Yoga Sutras of Patañjali'* to be one of the foundational texts of classical Yoga philosophy. Sutra in Indian literary traditions refers to an aphorism or a collection of aphorisms in the form of a manual or, more broadly, a condensed manual or text. Sutras are a genre of ancient and medieval Indian texts found in Hinduism, Buddhism and Jainism. In Buddhism, sutras, also known as suttas, are canonical scriptures, many of which are regarded as records of the oral teachings of Gautama Buddha.

Siddha is a term that is used widely in Indian religions and culture. It means *'one who is accomplished.'* It refers to perfected masters who have achieved a high degree of physical as well as spiritual perfection or enlightenment. In Jainism, the term is used to refer to the liberated souls. Siddha may also refer to one who has attained a siddhi, - paranormal capabilities.

Maharsi Patanjali, also a legendary Indian sage, in the third chapter of *'Yogi Sutra'*, says that while focusing on this coronal light, you can have a vision of siddhas, hence some practitioners of yoga say that while meditating at this area, they can see bright light, and they just enjoy being in that state. So the pineal gland for sure is no ordinary organ! It has a greater role to play in our metaphysical and spiritual dimension! And meditation can activate this organ to its full potential.

We use so much energy through our eyes, but here is a third eye which is observing what your eyes are looking at and what your mind is thinking about. It is our biological clock!

And here is where it all gets **very interesting! Very interesting** when we consider the shape of the pineal gland. Because what shape is the pineal gland? - It's pine-shaped! And what is so interesting about the pine shape?

We find references to the pineal gland in numerous ancient cultures in the form of a pine cone, - the ancient Sumerians gave the pineal gland the description of a pine cone. And we can see it in all the symbolism-encoded ancient art. Pine cones were associated with spiritual enlightenment by ancient Babylonians, Egyptians and Greeks. They represent the mysteries between the physical and spiritual worlds, the human brain and the pineal gland. Knowledge of sacred geometry focuses on the pineal gland. The pine cone staff is a symbol of the solar god Osiris and originated in Egypt where he was their messiah who died for his people and whose mother, Isis, was worshipped as the Egyptian version of the later Christian Virgin Mary. The Vatican has the world's largest pine cone that once decorated a fountain in ancient Rome next to a vast temple of Isis. The pope carries a pine cone mounted on his staff, where it symbolises rebirth and the sun. The pine is also the common symbol on images of Hindu gods in India and the Roman-Greek gods. The image of the solar god Osiris in the Egyptian museum in Turin in Italy, carries a pine cone.

So, as in all spiritual traditions, the *'vision'* of the third eye plays a fundamental role in the connection of the Spirit with man. In fact, it allows us to enter the *'non-material'* world, of the apparently invisible, through extra-sensorial perception, to bring us knowledge, deep awareness and *'guide'* our existence.

This is why it is so important to keep that pineal gland, - our third eye,- active and in a functional state. Due to the accumulation of toxins and heavy metals in the human body over time, such as fluoride, aluminium and mercury, the third eye becomes calcified, and gradually inactive. Hence the highlighting by activist groups of the dangers of the amount of fluoride that is being put into our waters! Fluoride is probably the element that most speeds up the decreasing functionality of our third eye. It is found in food products, and in such as toothpaste and mouthwashes, in chewing gum, and in fizzy drinks.

We can detoxify our body and take substances that promote the decalcification of the pineal gland. This is important because in order to achieve higher states of consciousness, toxins must first be cleansed from the body and one must become grounded to the energy of the earth. Opening or activating the third eye is a practice that anyone can do. It is not in any way dangerous, but like all spiritual practices, it takes time and cannot be hurried or forced. It is best done through meditation, with the focus totally on that area of the forehead.

Our ordinary human eyesight allows us only very limited vision of the totality of all that is actually around us, - probably only about 5%. It is our third eye that allows us to *'see'* the remaining 95%. The Egyptian pharaohs and priests of antiquity knew the importance of activating the pineal gland in order to reach higher states of conscious awareness.

And here is where it becomes even **more interesting! Much more interesting**!

Those PCR tests! Invasive probes that go so far past the upper sinus cavity that they can actually penetrate the blood brain barrier, dangerously close to the pineal gland. These ethyl oxide swabs deep inside people's delicate nasopharyngeal membranes! What are they collecting? Or, indeed, what are they delivering?

I do not know the answers, but I can question that if this was such a virulent virus, why would a drop of saliva not have been sufficient?

Is this all a deliberate attempt to dumb down our third eye vision? To disconnect us from higher states of consciousness? To prevent us from accessing those higher states of consciousness? To separate us from our soul? - Again I do not know the answers, but we do need to question!

Simply because we cannot forget about the chief instigator and promoter of that Covid-19 '*vaccination*' programme! Bill Gates! The same Bill Gates steeped in eugenics! Eugenics being the name given to the scientific planning of human breeding, initially and '*supposedly*' in order to improve the health of future generations. During the late 1920s and early 1930s, there was great enthusiasm for the possibility of using eugenics to assist in the creation of healthier people. However, as often happens with great causes, and with positive scientific advances, they can be taken over by the more negative elements. Science is all about discovering the truth, but sometimes that truth is deliberately kept hidden by those who wish to pervert it, for whatever reasons. And so eugenics came to be used as a means, not to improve the health of future generations and humanity in general, but to prevent the breeding of those who were deemed, by certain other people, to be inferior or undesirable for society. Eugenics became the premise of those people who believe the masses are too moronic or too ignorant to govern themselves. People targeted included, amongst others, epileptics, criminals, alcoholics, people with mental disabilities, members of racial minorities, members of the gay community and members of travelling communities.

And when we think of 'eugenics' as in select breeding and eradication of those termed 'undesirables', who, immediately springs to mind? Hitler! Yes, the very man! And after Hitler adopted these concepts from America and implemented an aggressive form of the concept, the world grew to take a different view of eugenics. Hitler himself stated:

'Anyone who interprets National Socialism merely as a political movement knows almost nothing about it. It is more than religion; it is the determination to create a new man.'

And put all of this alongside the fact that in 2010, Bill Gates committed $10 billion to the WHO promising to reduce population, in part, through new vaccines. A month later, Gates told a Ted Talk that new vaccines 'could reduce population'. In the same year, 2010, the Gates Foundation funded a trial of a GSK's experimental malaria vaccine, killing 151 African infants and causing serious adverse effects including paralysis, seizure, and febrile convulsions to 1,048 of the 5,049 children.

Yes, Gates has a history of vaccination promotion! He who has no medical qualifications or training of any sort! Gates the Micro-soft founder! Gates who claimed:

'This is not a vaccine story. This is a population management story.'

And an essential part of the recent 'vaccination' roll out programme was those PCR tests!

So should we be worried? Should we be concerned? Should we be asking questions? Especially now that the FIFTH vaccination for Covid-19 is being rolled out!

There is one thing for sure! - We need to WAKE UP!

CHAPTER 9:

Further down the rabbit hole

Let's go further down the rabbit hole!

We are eletromagnetic, biological units of consciousness, pure God essence, manifest in physical form, all vibrating on a particular energy vibration frequency, just like absolutely everything else in the totality of all creation.

And we live in a world, in a universe, held together by the vibrations of sound, colour, geometrical patterns, mathematical equations, numerical sequences, all inter-weaving, all inter-mingling, all inter-upholstering! An exquisite design, an exquisite tapestry in which we all weave our own thread. And all subject to the great Universal Laws. All part of the divine God Code.

The great Cosmic Dance! The great choreographed twirling and swirling! All moving to the harmonised note of the great cosmic orchestra! All sparkling and shimmering in the great kaleidoscope of colour! All synchronised in a finely-tuned balancing act! All perfection! All encoded within the great God Code!

Mathematical equations, numerical sequences, geometric designs, sound and colour vibrations, - all holding us together!

Numbers! Let us recall those famous words of Nikola Tesla, claiming that the numbers 3, 6 and 9 hold the keys to the Universe. How?

First of all in their shapes, - 3, 6 and 9 are each inherently embedded in the number 8, - the number 8, the only totally enclosed number with no opening or outlet, being the Infinity sign, the Lemniscate, wherein everything, absolutely everything is contained within the One Great Universal Flow of Energy, - that which we call God.

The number 3 is, in its shape, half of the number 8; the number 6 is, in its shape, the bottom part of the number 8 and the number 9 is, in its shape, the top half of the number 8. So 3, 6 and 9 are intrinsically embedded in the number 8.

And when you impose the number 8 over any other number, the number 8 still dominates, - all other numbers disappear into it. They are absorbed by the 8. And when you impose any other number on top of the 8, every other number melts into the 8, - the 8 is still the only number you can see.

So when Tesla claimed that 3, 6 and 9 are the keys to the Universe, what he meant was that 3, 6 and 9 all make up the shape of the number 8. So the number 8 is in fact the KEY TO THE UNIVERSE! All energy flows in the figure 8.

And there is something else Tesla meant! Something else to the 3, 6 and 9 numbers!

And it has to do with the power of sound! Sound is one of the purest forms of energy in existence. All sound is a vibration, affecting our own vibration level, by either raising it or lowering it.

And sound has the power and capacity to alter dense physical matter. An opera singer, for example, can shatter a crystal glass through the high frequency emitted by her voice. When the frequency of her voice reaches the level where it resonates with the frequency of the natural material essence of the glass, and that note is held long enough, it excites the vibrational field within the molecular structure of the glass, and then the glass simply shatters.

The Solfeggio Frequencies! Frequencies of sound! 6 Powerful Solfeggio Frequencies that raise our vibration! A series of 6 electromagnetic musical tones that the Gregorian Monks were said to use when they chanted in meditation. Rediscovered in 1974 by Dr. Joseph Puleo, the Solfeggio Frequencies are said to deeply penetrate the conscious and subconscious mind, stimulating inner healing. Dr. Puleo was intuitively led to rediscover these healing frequencies in the Book of Numbers - a book in the Hebrew Bible, - using a numerological technique to decipher the six repeating codes he found. The result was the rediscovery of the Solfeggio Frequencies.

And those same 3 numbers that Tesla spoke about - 3, 6 and 9. - Guess what!

These three numbers, 3, 6 and 9 - these same three numbers form the root vibration of the six Solfeggio Frequencies!

Here are the 6 Solfeggio Frequencies, and their effects, taken from Patricia Cori's book 'Hacking the God Code', page 279:

174 Hz - Reduce pain, alleviate stress

285 Hz - Influence energy, rejuvenation

396 Hz - Liberating guilt and fear

417 Hz - Facilitating change

528 Hz - Transformation and Miracles; DNA repair

639 Hz - Connecting; relationships

And now we need to go further down the rabbit hole to find the explanation for this!

Using the Pythagorean method of number and vibration, - all of which I explained in my previous book **'YOU'RE JUST A NUMBER! AND THE UNIVERSE HAS IT! ENCODED WITHIN THE GREAT COSMIC CODE'** published in 2022, - Dr. Puleo found that the original Solfeggio Frequencies, when reduced to their single base number, - they all end up as 3, 6 or 9.

For example, 174 Hz reduced to a single number is 1 + 7 + 4 = 12, and 1 + 2 = 3

285 Hz when reduced to its base number is 2 + 8 + 5 = 15, and 1 + 5 = 6

396 Hz reduces to 3 + 9 + 6 =18, and 1 + 8 = 9

And so on! And none of this can be coincidence, for there is no such thing! Just synchronicity! How all of creation is synchronised within the great God Code! All perfection!

The power of numbers! And there are those in our world who know all about it! Those in our world who know how to use the energy of numbers to their advantage!

Just look at the following:

World War One began on 28th July 1914 - That's 2 + 8 + 7 + 1 + 9 + 1 + 4 = 32. Reduced to a single digit this gives us 3 + 2 = 5.

World War Two began on 1st September 1939 - That's 1 + 9 + 1 + 9 + 3 + 9 = 32. Reduced to a single digit this gives us 3 + 2 = 5.

Putin invaded Ukraine on 24th February 2022 - That's 2 + 4 + 2 + 2 + 0 + 2 + 2 = 14. Reduced to a single digit, this gives us 1 + 4 = 5.

The Twin Towers in New York City were brought down on 11th September 2001 - That's 1 + 1 + 9 + 2 + 0 + 0 + 1 = 14. Reduced to a single digit, this gives us 1 + 4 = 5

And what about the flight numbers of those planes?

Flight American Airlines 11 - and as a Master number, this number is not reduced;

Flight United Airlines 93 which came down in Pennsylvania, 9 + 3 = 12;

Flight United Airlines 175 = 1 + 7 + 5 = 13;

Flight American Airlines 77 = 7 + 7 = 14;

Total 11 + 12 + 13 + 14 = 50. Reduced to a single digit, this gives us 5

And in the great God Code, what is the number 5 all about?

5 as a number has a fiery, ever-changing energy. 5 thrives on change and adventure to the extent of risk-taking. 5 is versatile, adaptable and resourceful. Where 3 is the energy causing change, 5 is the energy of change itself. Movement, action, drive and pushing for change are all in the positive energy of 5, but in the negative aspect, there can be impulsiveness, a tendency to force things rather than allowing synchronicity and the natural flow of the universal energy to guide us forward.

So it would appear to be very obvious that those who orchestrate such vile deeds all know about the power and significance of numbers!

And finally for this chapter, to further the number 8 as being the dominant number, the KEY TO THE UNIVERSE, let us look at the following tables:

8 x 1 = 8 = single digit 8

8 x 2 = 16 = single digit 1+ 6 = 7

8 x 3 = 24 = single digit 2 + 4 = 6

8 x 4 = 32 = single digit 3 + 2 = 5

8 x 5 = 40 = single digit 4 + 0 = 4

8 x 6 = 48 = single digit 4 + 8 = 12 and 1 + 2 = 3

8 x 7 = 56 = single digit 5 + 6 = 11 and 1 + 1 = 2

8 x 8 = 64 = single digit 6 + 4 = 10 and 1 + 0 = 1

8 x 9 = 72 = single digit 7 + 2 = 9

8 x 10 =80 = single digit 8

8 x 11 = 88 = single digit 8 + 8 = 16 and 1 + 6 = 7

8 x 12 = 96 = single digit 9 + 6 =15 and 1 + 5 = 6

And so the sequence continues indefinitely starting with 8: - 8, 7, 6, 5, 4, 3, 2, 1, 9, 8, 7, 6, 5, 4, 3, 2, 1, 9, 8, 7, 6, 5, 4, 3, 2, 1 etc

See the structure that the number 8 imposes on all other numbers? The number 8 rules the proverbial roost!

And how about 3, 6 and 9?

The number 9, no matter how many multiples of that number are involved, you still end up with the root digit 9.

If you do the same multiplication table for the number 3, than you get the sequence 3, 6, 9, 3, 6, 9, 3, 6, 9, 3, 6, 9, etc

And with the number 6 in the multiplication table, you get the sequence 6, 3, (6 x 2=12, single digit 1 + 2 = 3) 9, 6, 3, 9, 6, 3, 9, 6, 3, 9, 6, 3, etc.

WE DID NOT INVENT NUMBERS, - WE DISCOVERED THEM!

All within the great God Code!

And the number 8 holds the key to the entire cosmos! What Tesla was telling us! The number 3, 6 and 9 being inherently embedded in the 8, - the Infinity sign, - encompassing THE ALL, - THE TOTALITY OF ALL THAT IS!

We need to WAKE UP to the power of numbers! And to the amazing and mind-boggling perfection of the God Code encoded in absolutely everything and everyone throughout all of Creation!

Chapter 10:

Robo Sapiens, - the invisible enemy!

We have just seen how our world, our universe and all of Creation is held together in the most delicate, the most finely tuned balance, the most intricately woven tapestry of sound, colour, mathematical equations, numerical frequencies and geometrical designs. Everything is encoded within the great, all-encompassing God Code. All tuned to perfection!

And that includes each and every one of us! Each one of us is a microcosm of the macrocosm of the entirety of Creation. And as such, each and every one of us is encoded with the God Code.

Perfection! Remember how Shakespeare's Hamlet described man:

'What a piece of work is man! How noble in reason! How infinite in faculty! In form and moving how express and admirable! In action how like an angel! In apprehension how like a god! The beauty of the world! The paragon of animals!'

So why would anyone want to change or tamper with what we are? But, unfortunately for humanity, there are those who do! There are those who wish to push science along the negative path, right to the very boundaries where we can no longer identify ourselves as being humans, - but more as a machine. Stripped of all that makes us unique, - our very soul, - we respond like robots to those who programme the AI systems. *'That's all just science fiction',* I hear you shout, *'That's never going to happen!'*

154

Well, you just keep telling yourself that! But I am telling you, it is already happening! The robot age is upon us!

WAKE UP!

'Robosapiens' is the name of a toy-like biomorphic robot designed by Mark Tilden and produced by WowWee toys. The *'Robosapien X'* was made to entertain and will react to sounds and touch. The *'Robosapien'* is preprogrammed with moves, and also can be controlled by an infrared remote control included with the toy, or by either a personal computer equipped with an infrared PDA. The robot's remote control unit has a total of 21 different buttons. With the help of two shift buttons, a total of 67 different robot-executable commands are accessible.

The *'toy'* is capable of a walking motion without recourse to wheels within its feet. It can grasp objects with either of its hands, and throw grasped objects. It has a small loudspeaker unit, which can broadcast several different vocalisations. Released in 2004, the product sold over 1.5 million units between April and December in that year.

Experts now say that children should be taught about the risks of artificial intelligence from the moment they get their first mobile phone, because the robot age is upon us. Although Terminator-style killer cyborgs remain - for now - on the pages of science fiction books, technology is already sufficiently advanced to impact all areas of our lives.

The speed of the breakthroughs has even shocked tech leaders, with more than 1,000, including Elon Musk and Apple co-founder Steve Wozniak, urging companies to pause further research. And as this book goes to press, Sam Tonkin for MAILONLINE published the following, 2nd May 2023:

'The 'Godfather' of AI quits Google job amid fears tyrants like Putin could use the growing intelligence of robots for 'bad things' - as bitter Silicon Valley civil war over dangers of the tech rages on. Some of world's greatest minds are split over whether AI is a good or bad thing. British-Canadian pioneer Geoffrey Hinton issued stern warning about dangers.

The 'godfather' of artificial intelligence (AI) has tossed a grenade into the raging debate about the dangers of the technology — after sensationally quitting his job at Google and saying he regrets his life's work. British-Canadian pioneer Geoffrey Hinton, 75, further fanned the flames of a growing Silicon Valley civil war, as he issued a spine-chilling warning that 'scary' chatbots like the hugely popular ChatGPT could soon become smarter than humans. Some of the world's greatest minds are split over whether AI will destroy or elevate humanity, with Microsoft billionaire Bill Gates championing the technology and Tesla founder Elon Musk a staunch critic, saying he fears AI will no longer listen to humans. The bitter argument spilled into the public domain earlier this year when more than 1,000 tech tycoons signed a letter calling for a pause on the 'dangerous race' to advance AI. They said urgent action was needed before humans lose control of the technology and risk being wiped out by robots.'

And what more has been confirmed? -

Stephen Hawking believed it could spell the end of the human race. Geoffrey Hinton as we have just read, worries that *'bad actors'* such as Putin could use AI for *'bad things',* by programming robots to *'get more power'.* Apple co-founder Steve Wozniak Says AI has the potential to make *'horrible mistakes'.*

Supporters argue, however, that AI may be a brilliant thing for civilisation because it could help cure cancer, solve climate change, and eradicate poverty.

But Dr. Hinton, the British-Canadian cognitive psychologist and computer scientist, as we have just seen, has resigned over it, due to the profound risks to society and to humanity, and he sounds the alarm about the dangers of how quickly AI is advancing. He said chatbots are already capable of holding more general knowledge than a human brain, and added that it is only a matter of time before AI also eclipses us when it comes to reasoning. Dr. Hinton's ground-breaking research on deep learning and neural networks has laid the foundations for current AI technology, but he cautioned that humanity should now be 'worried' about the consequences of developing these systems further:

'Right now, they're not more intelligent than us, as far as I can tell. But I think they soon may be'.

Industry experts said Dr. Hinton's announcement was a 'significant moment for the future of AI that had caught the world's attention'.

Jake Moore, global cyber security adviser at ESET, said: 'Although we are a little way off computers attacking humans, bad actors are already taking advantage of the power of this technology to aid them in their attacks.......We have spent many years investing in AI but this wonderful achievement will inevitably be used nefariously and could form part of larger scale attacks, especially if used in nation state attacks.'

What are the dangers? Fears about AI come as experts predict it will achieve singularity by 2045, which is when the technology surpasses human intelligence and we cannot control it.

Dr Carissa Veliz, an associate professor in AI at the University of Oxford, added: 'That so many experts are speaking up about their concerns regarding the safety of AI, with some computer scientists going as far as regretting some of their work, should alarm policymakers. The time to regulate AI is now.'

Elon Musk, Apple co-founder Steve Wozniak and the late Stephen Hawking are among the most famous critics of AI, who believe the technology poses a *'profound risk to society and humanity'* and could have *'catastrophic'* effects.

And Eric Schmidt, former CEO of Google, said:

'AI has the potential to harm or kill many, many people in the near future'.

He expressed his concern about the *'existential risk'* of the rapidly evolving technology and warned that it will be difficult to contain. An *'existential risk'* being defined as many, many, many people harmed or killed.

However, Bill Gates, Google CEO Sundar Pichai and futurist Ray Kurzweil are on the other side of the debate. They think ChatGPT- like AI could be the *'most important'* innovation of our time.

Also among those to sign the letter asking for a pause were scientists John Hopfield from Princeton University and Rachel Branson, of the Bulletin of Atomic Scientists, as well as DeepAI founder Kevin Baragona. Barogona explained why the rapidly advancing field of AI was so dangerou: *'It's almost akin to a war between chimps and humans,'* he told DailyMail.com:

'The humans obviously win since we're far smarter and can leverage more advanced technology to defeat them......If we're like the chimps, then the AI will destroy us, or we'll become enslaved to it.'

Bill Gates believes the rise of AI is poised to improve humanity, increase productivity, reduce worldwide inequalities and accelerate the development of - what else? - New vaccines! Surprise! Surprise!

The systems, which include machine learning and deep learning sub-fields, are made up of AI algorithms that seek to create expert systems which make predictions or classifications based on input data. From 1957 to 1974, AI flourished. Computers could store more information and became faster, cheaper, and more accessible. Machine learning algorithms also improved and people got better at knowing which algorithm to apply to their problem. Now with the release of ChatGPT at the end of last year, its popularity and what it can achieve is evidence of how fast the technology is growing.

The chatbot is a large language model trained on massive text data, allowing it to generate eerily human-like text in response to a given prompt. In just a few months, it has passed the Bar exam with a higher score than 90 per cent of humans who have taken it, and it achieved 60 per cent accuracy on the US Medical Licensing Exam. People have also used ChatGPT to write research papers, books, news articles, emails and other text-based work.

However, while some see the chatbot and others like it as a virtual assistant of the future, many others worry it could signal the beginning of the end for humanity. With Dr Hinton's resignation, the debate is only likely to intensify.

And so far, there have been some scary developments!

Obvious incarnations of AI technology include deep fakes - computer-generated photos and videos which use face recognition technology to replicate a person's face or body. An image of Pope Francis, - and which the public believed to be real, - wearing a shiny white puffer jacket, a long chain with a cross and a water bottle in his hand was created by image-generator Midjourney, which was also behind the fake scenes of Donald Trump being arrested by police officers in New York City. Deepfake videos have also shown the evil powers of AI, allowing users to create clips of public figures spreading misinformation - and experts predict 90 percent of online content will be made this way by 2025. Web culture expert Ryan Broderick said the pope image was *the first real mass-level AI misinformation case*. And Bellingcat journalist Eliot Higgins created the images this month, showing Trump being chased down the street by police officers while his wife Melania screams. Others show the former President in jail wearing an orange jumpsuit.

These scary AI developments seem to be just the tip of the iceberg. Deepfake videos and images have also seen a boom online, showing influential figures relaying misinformation. Currently, no laws protect humans from being generated into a digital form by AI.

Professor Stuart Russell, one of those 1,000 experts who last month signed an open letter calling for a six-month pause in the development of AI systems, speaking to Sky's Sophy Ridge, explained why he signed:

'I signed it because I think it needs to be said that we don't understand how these more powerful systems work. We don't know what they're capable of. And that means that we can't control them, we can't get them to behave themselves...... People were concerned about disinformation, about racial and gender bias in the outputs of these systems'.

And he argued with the swift progression of AI, time was needed to *'develop the regulations that will make sure that the systems are beneficial to people rather than harmful'.*

Russell said one of the biggest concerns was disinformation and deep fakes - videos or photos of a person in which their face or body has been digitally altered so they appear to be someone else - typically used maliciously or to spread false information. Even though disinformation has been around for a long time for *'propaganda'* purposes, the difference now is that, using Sophy Ridge as an example, he could ask GPT-4 to try to *'manipulate'* her so she's *'less supportive of Ukraine'.* The technology would read Ridge's social media presence and what she has ever said or written, and then carry out a gradual campaign to *'adjust'* her news feed.

Professor Russell told Ridge: *'The difference here is I can now ask GPT-4 to read all about Sophy Ridge's social media presence, everything Sophy Ridge has ever said or written, all about Sophy Ridge's friends and then just begin a campaign gradually by adjusting your news feed, maybe occasionally sending some fake news along into your news feed so that you're a little bit less supportive of Ukraine, and you start pushing harder on politicians who say we should support Ukraine in the war against Russia and so on.'*

Will this chatbot replace humans? Russell's response:

'That will be very easy to do. And the really scary thing is that we could do that to a million different people before lunch.'

Ridge described it as *'genuinely really scary'* and asked if that kind of thing was happening now, to which the professor replied: *'Quite likely, yes.'*

He said China, Russia and North Korea have large teams who *'pump out disinformation'* and with AI *'we've given them a power tool'.*

'The concern of the letter is really about the next generation of the system. Right now the systems have some limitations in their ability to construct complicated plans.'

An expert, who is a professor of computer science at the University of California, Berkeley, warned of *'a huge impact with these systems for the worse by manipulating people in ways that they don't even realise is happening.'*

Elon Musk suggested under the next generation of systems, or the one after that, corporations could be run by AI systems, - *'You could see military campaigns being organised by AI systems...*

If you're building systems that are more powerful than human beings, how do human beings keep power over those systems forever? That's the real concern behind the open letter.'

Professor David Yeng of Harvard University has recently stated:

'AI is fundamentally a technology for prediction and autocratic governments would like to be able to predict the whereabouts, thoughts, and behaviours of citizens...... If China successfully exports its technology, it could generate a spreading of similar autocratic regimes to the rest of the world.'

Professor Cai Hengjin, of the AI Research Institute at China's Wuhan University, said: *'One measurement is how fast and powerful AI would grow beyond our imagination......Some thought it would grow slowly and we still have decades or even hundreds of years left - but that's not the case. We only have a couple of years - because our AI advancement is just too fast.'*

Expert Professor Mark Lee, from Birmingham University, said while killer robots may be decades away, we should be more concerned about the here and now. The tech race, he believes, is *'unstoppable'* - meaning *'we should prepare for a new age'.*

Just after Russia's invasion of Ukraine last year, the Kremlin showed how this war would be different by generating a deep fake video purporting to show Ukrainian President Volodymyr Zelensky ordering his troops to surrender.

The same technology now allows scammers to replicate the voice of loved ones and launch fake calls claiming there is an emergency and asking for money. All it takes is a few seconds of video to generate a near-perfect match of someone's voice. And we are now constantly being warned!

'It takes effort and resources to employ banks of trolls - but imagine when autocratic governments are able to do this using AI..............There is no real sense that these multinationals know where they're going with these developments as they race against each other to secure the next hit', said Professor Lee.

And he added:

'Since it cannot be stopped, the only answer is education..........We have

to teach people how to evaluate information, question information. It will require education in critical rethinking and scientific method and it will have to begin as soon as you give your kids their first mobile phone and they encounter AI for the first time.'

We saw earlier in this book how films and movies are all a form of propaganda and brain washing. So we need to ask, - are we being prepared through movies for this new generation of Robo Sapiens? Movies such as '*A Space Odyssey'; 'Star Wars*'; '*Blade Runner'; 'The Terminator'; 'AI: Artificial Intelligence'; 'I, Robot'; and 'M3GHAN'* (2022). These are just a very few of the movies that are and have been hitting our screens over the last number of decades. Preparing us for?

WAKE UP!

'*Robo Sapiens - Evolution of a New Species*' is also the title of a book by Peter Menzel and Faith D'Alusio. Menzel is a photographer known for his coverage of international feature stories on science and the environment. His award-winning photographs have been published in '*Life', 'National Geographic', 'Smithsonian',* the '*New York Times Magazine' 'Time', 'GEO'* and '*Le Figaro'.* Faith D'Alusio is a former television news producer. Her documentary and news series pieces have won regional and national awards from the Headlines Foundation, United Press International, Associated Press, and the Radio-Television News Directors Association.

Reviews for their book include:

'This is one of the most mind-stretching - and frightening - books I have ever read. It's also a tour de force of photography: the images reveal a whole new order of creation about to come into existence. No one who

has any interest in the future can afford to miss it.' (Sir Arthur C. Clarke)

'An engaging and insightful compendium illuminating our accelerating ascent to the inevitable merger of human and machine. Although many today find the prospect disconcerting, by the time the Robo Sapiens are fully amongst us, we will find it very natural to interact intimately with these inventions of our intellect.' (Ray Kurtzwell, recipient of the 1999 National Medal of Technology and author of *'The Age of Spiritual Machines: When Computers Exceed Human Intelligence.'*)

'You pick up Robo Sapiens for the great photos, and then get caught up reading the inside politics of the race to build humanlike machines. Don't be surprised by the coming era of robotics - read Robo Sapiens and be ready.' (K. Eric Drexler, Chairman, Foresight Institute, and author of *'Engines of Creation and Nanosystems')*

So what is the book about? It is a guide to our mechanical future! The authors present the next generation of intelligent robots and their makers. Accompanying brilliant photographs of more than a hundred robots are extensive interviews with robotic pioneers, anecdotal field notes with behind-the-scenes information and easy-to-understand technical data about the machines.

Around the world, scientists and engineers are participating in a high-stakes race to build the first intelligent robot. Many robots already exist - automobile factories are full of them. But the new generation of robots will be something else: smart machines that act ever more like living creatures.

What will happen then? With our prosthetic limbs, titanium hips, and artificial eyes, we are already beginning to resemble our machines. And when we implant chips in our bodies to connect ourselves directly to computers, the likeness will become only more pronounced. Science fiction will have become science fact.

Meanwhile - and equally important - our machines are beginning to resemble us. Robotic spiders, crabs, geckos, and dogs are already spilling from the laboratories. The next steps are to re-create Homo Sapiens itself and then go beyond. Robots can already walk, talk and dance; they can react to human facial expressions and obey verbal commands. When scientists go on to create fully autonomous robots with greater intelligence than human beings, will they be our partners or our rivals? Will it be simply a robotic revolution or a true extension of evolution? Could machines and humankind meld into a single species - *Robo sapiens*?

In the introduction to the book, Menzel writes|:

'Before Faith and I began this book, I would have attributed the term 'Robo sapiens' to a science-fiction writer. I would have been amused but would have scoffed especially hard at those modifiers 'vastly superior', and 'dominant' in its (admittedly hypothetical) definition. I have been skeptical about technology's undelivered promises ever since I began a career as a photojournalist, more than two decades ago. More specifically, I am skeptical not about technology per se but about the way scientists misuse and misunderstand it. Nuclear power, for example, is a wonderful technology that would have had a prominent place in any wise, far-seeing, and incorruptible society. In the future, I hope to encounter such a society.

Pessimism about society's potential to misuse technology is nothing new. Czech writer Karel Capek coined the term 'robot' in a play he wrote in 1920 called 'R.U.R', first performed in 1923. The play's dark plot revolves around a factory - Rossum's Universal Robots, the R.U.R. of the title - that populates the world with artificial slaves, meant to relieve humans of the drudgery of work. Built in ever-increasing numbers and with an expanding intelligence, they soon outnumber their human masters, and then they are used as soldiers. Eventually, a robot revolt wipes out the human race. It's interesting that the person who invented the modern concept of robots predicted that they would destroy us all.'

And he continues:

'Another part of this puzzle is provided by the silicon chip, which has rammed our technological future into overdrive. Computers, nearly ubiquitous now, soon will be. Every year, they get smaller, faster, cheaper, and more powerful. According to what is known as Moore's Law, computer chips will become faster and more powerful by a factor of two every year or so. This exponential increase shows no sign of abating. Contrast this with the evolution of the human brain and many experts conclude that machine intelligence will inevitably surpass human intelligence - the only question, is what will happen when it does.

These are the unknowns in the equation that make the future exciting and possibly a bit scary - they blur the lines between science and philosophy. Since we don't understand the basis for human consciousness yet, how can we create it in machines? Or will mechanical minds start up by themselves when they reach a certain level of complexity?'

So will we lose some of our humanity? Will we lose the poverty, fear, and desperation that has always been the human lot? - Possibly! Or will we destroy ourselves? - Equally possibly!

Menzel spells it out:

'But in either case, the RoboCup of 2050 begins not with humans and robots facing off, but with both sides standing together. The players, each a different combination of person and machine, shake hands. In the noise and glare of the crowd, one can imagine it being hard to tell them apart. They line up, indistinguishable from afar, on either side of the midfield line, metal and flesh, flesh and metal, all in an inextricable tangle.

The spectators' shout reaches a crescendo as the first foot touches the ball. It is the first whisper of evolution, the dawn of a new species: Robo sapiens.'

And no, it's not all bad news! The advances in technology are certainly bringing hope to humanity. Just think of the countless numbers of people who have benefited from and are alive today because of the innovations in technology and machines.

BUT! It is the way in which those working in the negative energy fields misuse it and push for control of humanity, - by changing the God Code! Playing God with the finely tuned beings that we are! Restructuring humanity along artificial, false principles. Merging our DNA with machines! Making us all into robots, obeying commands from a central control point! Is this what we want for our next generation?

There is no enemy more threatening than an invisible one! And surely AI is our invisible enemy!

WAKE UP!

Eileen McCourt

Conclusion

Mark Passio, independent researcher, public speaker, radio talk show host, conference organiser and freedom activist from Philadelphia wrote:

'There are only two mistakes you can make on the path to truth. One is not starting, the other is not going the whole way.'

We as humans, are living now in the most extraordinary of times, as humanity ascends to higher vibration consciousness levels. As humanity makes the enormous transition, the great shift, from the old, controlling ideological ideals and values based on religion and religious beliefs, to an expansion of human consciousness, innovation and science.

But there are those who do not wish this to happen! There are those who are steeped in darkness, - in the greed of materialism and power. In the negative clutch of the ego. Those who influence and control mainstream media, - leading us to a perception of our world as a hostile, violent and barbaric place. Those who seem to be determined to lead our world down a disastrous course to destruction and annihilation. Those who seem determined to change us from biological beings into some form of transhumanist robots. Those who seek to detach us from our soul, from Spirit, from Source. Those who seek to mutate the biological beings that we are, into some sort of soulless creatures, - for whatever purpose. Those who seek to hold back our awareness and evolutionary process, - for whatever reason.

Probably because they desire above all else to retain control. And hence we are being manipulated through their use of the most lethal of all weapons - fear!

There is no doubt about it! - There is a battle going on between the forces of good and the darker forces. A battle for the soul of humanity! And make no mistake! - The dark energy forces are strong! Very strong! And they have an agenda that is not for the benefit or the good of humanity! *What if* that agenda is to isolate the God-Code inherent within each one of us? *What if* that agenda is to isolate, remove and then replace that God-Code inherent within each one of us with some sort of mechanical code or some overriding alternative vibrational sequence? *What if* this process is already well under way? - As the evidence indeed suggests!

I do not know the answers! But at least I can ask questions! And hopefully through this book, get others to think!

And the good news is, - the agenda of the darker energy forces is no longer working! No longer working as they had planned! Take for example, their plan to have us all issued with a vaccination passport by now! That never happened!

And why not? Simply because *we are messing up their plans*! So many millions of people all across the world have awakened to what is going on, and millions more are awakening every day. And as more and more people WAKE UP, the great change for the better of humanity is really happening! And as *'they'* try to go after us even harder and further, their entire plan is falling apart! It's actually all working now in our favour! The harder they try, the more it backfires on them, the more obvious their *game* becomes!

They cannot succeed. The forces of darkness cannot survive in the Light!

The LIght will always transmute the dark! That's the great Universal Law! Indisputable! Irrefutable! Inviolate! And the more Light we send out, the more darkness we transmute! So we need to **up our game**!

We are the ones we have been waiting for!

So what do we do? - Very simple really!

We need to stop engaging with the propaganda of all those programmes shoved out to us through social media! Turn it all off! Do not buy into all that social media propaganda that is aimed at sending us down a certain path! Be aware that any decision you may make that is based on any of their propaganda is deterministic and limiting. Take back your power! And as they continue to hold onto their power, we will see them turn the volume up! Banking dramas, maybe even a halt on international travel, - whatever it is they will try! But remember, - there is a lot that they tried, and a lot that we were afraid of, but which failed to happen! So their plans are definitely being messed up! And **we are the ones who are messing them up**! And we are messing them up because we are understanding their whole mechanism! We are seeing through this whole nonsense!

And as more and more revelations come, we as humanity are expanding our awareness, expanding our consciousness, because we are getting to the truth! And these revelations will continue, - simply **because there is nothing hidden that will not be revealed.**

Remember how Shakespeare's Hamlet described man:

'What a piece of work is man! How noble in reason! How infinite in faculty! In form and moving how express and admirable! In action how like an angel! In apprehension how like a god! The beauty of the world!

The paragon of animals!'

Each and every one of us is imbued with the God-Code. Sovereign beings, our true essence the God Essence. Our multidimensional consciousness what ultimately defines our existence here on this planet.

And we cannot allow that God-Code to be interfered with! That delicate balance of sound, colour, mathematical equations, numerical sequences and geometric designs. A uniquely and finely tuned universe, so precise and perfect, that to disturb any part of it will bring destruction to it all.

And AI will do just that, - if we allow it! And how do we prevent it?

We WAKE UP!

Other Books by Eileen McCourt

Eileen has written 43 other books, including her first audio-book. All are available on Amazon. For more information, visit her author page:

www.eileenmccourt.co.uk

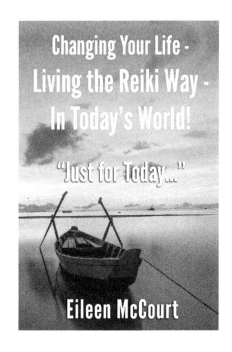

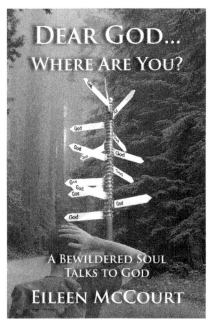

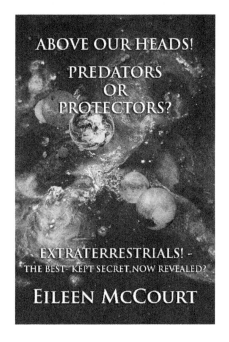

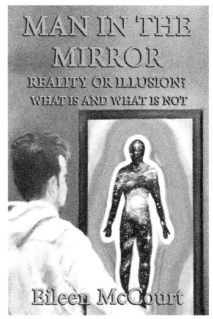

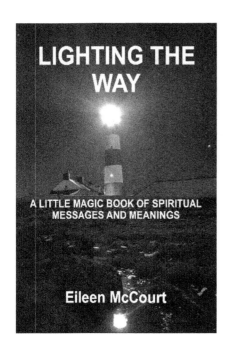

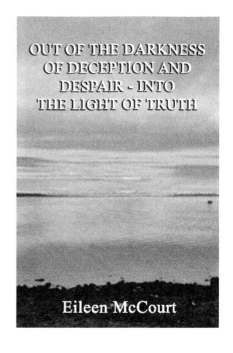

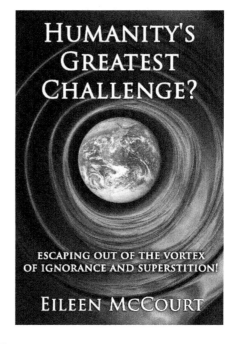

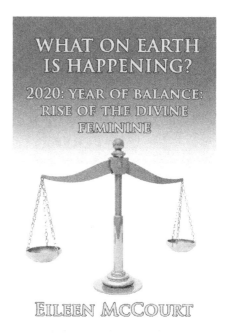

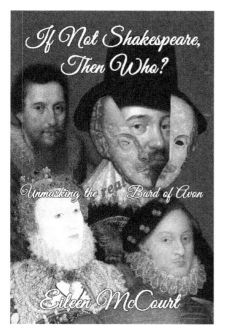

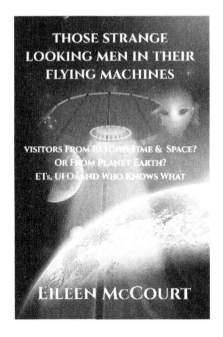

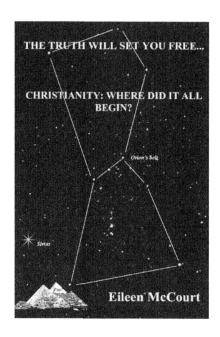

Audiobook

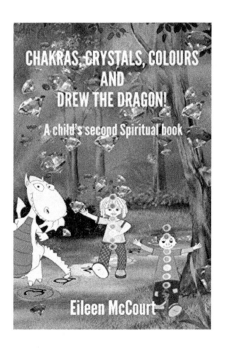

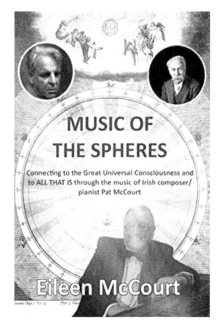

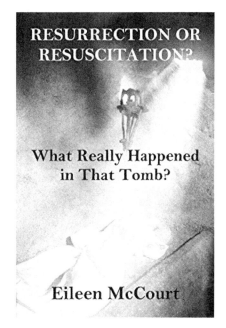

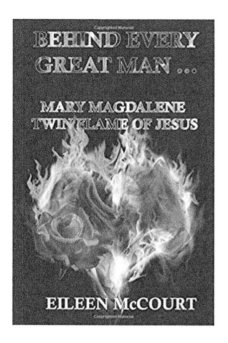

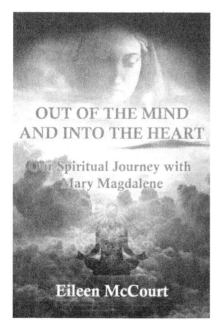

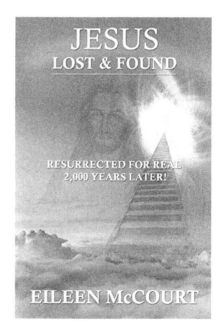

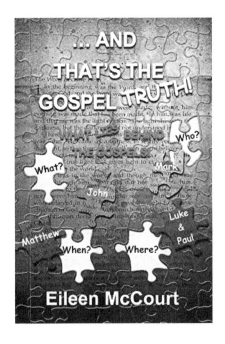

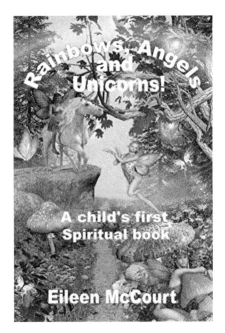

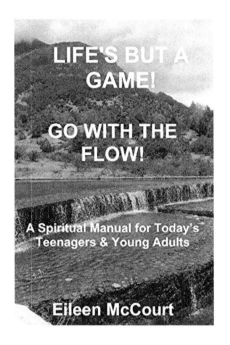

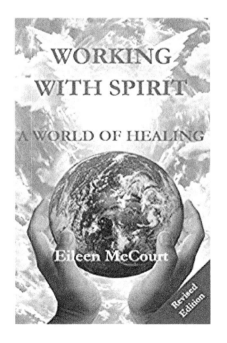

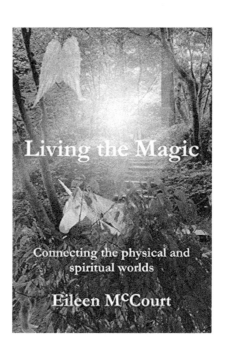

Living the Magic

Connecting the physical and spiritual worlds

Eileen McCourt

184

Printed in Great Britain
by Amazon

23047087R00119